Without Prejudice

Published by:
Written by: Roger Murray M.D. and Toby Unwin M.B.A

ISBN number: 0-9729814-0-3
Library of congress control number(PCN): 2003103245

Visit: www.PracticeWithoutFear.com

Also by the authors:
The Flake Filter – How to spot flaky people before they waste your time - Toby Unwin
Papers and books previously published by Roger Murray M.D. are of a medical nature and not relevant to this subject.

Disclaimer

The material presented in this book is presented for information purposes only. You should always do your own research and consult an appropriately qualified professional prior to taking any action which you do not understand fully. The legality of methods described in this book may vary with state, jurisdiction, time and interpretation. As with everything in life you are ultimately on your own here so double check everything. Suppliers and service provider's details listed in this book are given for information purposes only and do not constitute a recommendation.

Foreword

By Frank Steig M.D. J.D.

By their nature doctors fix things; they make things better. We are trained to recognize and treat disease, malady and injury(and no matter when or where and how likely it may be to interfere with our own comfort and convenience). Explaining what we do, and why we do it is something we learn early on in our experience as a doctor, to keep to ourselves; no one outside the profession can(or will) understand. Our skills, our arts, are practiced skillfully and unselfishly, beyond the true understanding or appreciation of those on the outside of the circle of the doctor. Usually, "it" works best that way; our families, our friends, our patients – virtually all of society – permit and even encourage us to do our good works, without the need to actually understand at all why we do what we do(or certainly how). Oh, they may converse and flirt with the "romance" of "being a doctor", and even sit for hours watching a television drama about the "true life" adventure of medicine; but they certainly are unwilling(and quite honestly, incapable) of getting down and dirty with what it really takes to do the job. And, "the job" in reality is more a calling and a quest than a neat and tidily bundled "occupation".

So then comes the dreaded assault of LIABILITY. Doctors are comfortable with the concept and burden of "responsibility". It was driven deep within our professional being from hour upon hour of "rounds" with peer and mentor, and grueling sessions of "mortality and morbidity" conferences. We take responsibility, learn from the mistakes that befall us, and go on to continually do better from that point forward. LIABILITY neither helps nor speeds on our quest. It is an external fetter that permits a ransom release from responsibility and produces no lesson that allows any forward motion or worthwhile opportunity to learn or improve. It becomes the response of those on the outside of the hallowed realms of our profession to "cash in" on the very life blood responsibility that keeps our calling of doctor sound and true. And unfortunately, it entices us to abrogate the collective responsibility of our profession(to "police it's own") for the quick and easy path of monetary ransom(the annual fee of our malpractice policy).

In business, management of loss and liability is an important consideration. All possible risks that face any particular business must be considered so that assets and sources of income can be protected – this is the basic concept of "loss exposure". Once this analysis of possible liability to the assets and income of the business(oftentimes and assessment of what can happen to whom as it relates to the property and operations of the business), then and estimation of "loss potential" can be made. This estimate of the maximum loss that the business may incur permits an intelligent determination of the risk that business must guard against in order to function. That "loss potential" may be addressed with the purchase of liability insurance, the creating of a self-insurance fund, or by choosing to place the business "at risk" by not protecting against the identified loss potential. In Health Care, legislative enactments generally require at least some minimum of loss potential protection(e.g. mandatory financial responsibility laws).

Unlike most other businesses, loss exposure for a physician may well exceed the magnitude of the assets and income of the business. With out-of-control jury verdicts reaching the multi-million dollar range, a single "bad outcome" could generate an award far exceeding the lifetime income of a single doctor. "Loss potential" for any doctor then may be well beyond the reach of any commercial malpractice or self-insurance plan.

Practice Without Fear becomes an essential educational building block for ALL doctors. It provides a primer to help us identify the disease entities associated with "liability" as well as many well-outlined treatments and important preventative measures to ease the sting of this liability malady. More importantly, *Practice Without Fear* may just prove to be the vaccination required to help eradicate the scourge of medical malpractice devastation from our society.

Frank Steig M.D. J.D.

Contents

Dedicated

To all the American physicians who have endured far more legal abuse and fear than anyone should, still remaining dedicated to medicine and patient advocacy. We hope that the information here will set you free, so that you can

Practice without fear.

Acknowledgements

We would like to thank Joelle and Julie, our partners for their endless patience, encouragement and enduring support in bringing this book to fruition. We would like to thank Jack Dicks J.D. esq. for reading the manuscript and making many helpful decisions that have enabled us to produce a much clearer treatise that this otherwise would have been without his help. Dr Martin Osment L.L.D. has helped us immeasurably in providing the knowledge of real world application of law that surpasses the skills of most attorneys.

Peter Holt provided us with a valuable insight into medical risk from the insurer's point of view. Sebastian Gault C.F.A. M.B.A. was very helpful in making the book more readable and suggesting the asset comparison charts. Earl Ratliff provided some, much needed, editorial input(it's amazing how difficult it is to catch your own mistakes). We would like to thank all the physicians who have contributed their personal experiences, tragedies and triumphs both personally and professionally to the making of this book. We would also like to thank them for the many useful recommendations of service providers.

1.Why you need asset protection?

Time saver tip: You should already know this, after all you bought the book. If you're short on time do yourself a favor and skip ahead to the end of the chapter because we're not going to be telling you anything you don't already know here.

Being a physician today sucks. When you started off in medical school it promised a safe, steady income. You were respected and knew you could always earn good, dependable money anywhere you went in the country. Now ambulance chasing attorneys run television adverts questioning your honesty, integrity, professional competence and inviting your patients to sue you.

The costs associated with excessive litigation are the cancer that afflicts our healthcare system. These are passed on throughout the chain, harming doctor, patient and facility alike. Ludicrous jury awards have no affect on the quality of patient care, but merely serve to increase the ever rising malpractice insurance premiums and line the pockets of greedy lawyers. 0.1% of the population and a few lawyers have become incredibly wealthy at the expense of the rest.

Unfortunately a number of doctors are now deciding that enough is enough and are either not performing high risk procedures, or are stopping practicing medicine altogether. The highest risk professions are currently:

- Emergency Room Care
- Obstetrics
- Radiology and Diagnostics, especially mammography
- Surgery, especially neurosurgery, pediatric neurosurgery and vascular surgery
- Orthopedics, especially back surgery

Many hospitals are having to stop offering procedures and refer their patients out of the area due to the lack of physicians willing to accept the risk of practicing.

The number of malpractice insurers is also dropping as the premiums(even though skyrocketing) cannot keep pace with the astronomical level of payouts. Insurance coverage will not only cost more this year, it may not be available to you.

The situation is exacerbated by falling reimbursements from insurers, governments and managed care companies. Uncollectible receivables combined with rising costs and labor shortages are pushing many practices out of business.

There needs to be drastic changes in our current system, and we address some basic advances at the end of this book. One thing is certain – if the status quo continues, the medical profession and ultimately, the patient can only suffer.

We all know that as physicians only another physician can really evaluate a complex case. Why do lawyers typically pick high school educated, left wing democrats to understand their insane arguments and produce verdicts accordingly?

You hear the mantra everywhere: TV, radio, bill boards, talk shows, basketball games, newspapers, Yellow Pages, etc. "If in doubt sue. If you're not sure then give us a call, well take a look at your case. If you're not entirely satisfied with the results of a procedure… If your doctor didn't inform you… Then call your local lawyer and get yourself some easy cash".

This sad message leaps out at you from every media outlet and doctors are being sued like never before. The saddest thing about this country is that people refuse to take individual responsibility for their own actions. They are encouraged to believe that everything is someone else's fault and the other person OWES them and should pay.

So what if you're morbidly obese, don't exercise and tuck away half a dozen Big Mac meals each day. It's your doctor's fault that you're fat – you have the right to perfect health. Why don't you sue them, you could get some money and it would absolve you of the responsibility to do anything about your own problems.

Lawyers will chase the doctor with the deepest pockets, guilt doesn't factor into it, not when physician's insurance companies carry tens of millions of dollars in malpractice coverage and will settle without looking at the evidence just so they don't have to roll the dice in a courtroom.

And why not, in court paid "experts"(medical prostitutes) will testify that black is white and right is wrong if the check clears. The jury doesn't know the difference, twelve of your "peers" with no medical training are expected to adjudicate on the rest of your life, your assets, and your professional reputation. You've got lots of money and look at that poor, unfortunate defendant, you're going to pay…

It reminds me of a joke…

A lady gets into a car accident. The policeman asks her is she's seriously injured. "How should I know, I'm a doctor, not a lawyer".

It's funny because it's true. It's also pretty sad. Apparently there are only three lawyer jokes – the rest are true stories.

Lawyers view doctors as their personal ATMs. If you're in practice today it's a matter of when, not if you're going to be sued. In our physician recruitment firm we see legal case history summaries appended to curriculum vitaes as a matter of course.

The situation in our state of Florida for malpractice insurance is catastrophic. Premiums have gone through the roof with some high risk specialties like OB's paying over $300K a year in premiums. These guys are the "lucky" ones, many neurosurgeons are giving up doing procedures entirely because they can't get insured. The number of malpractice insurers has dropped to three. None of them are taking on new clients and they are dropping many of their old ones.

Doctors are also usually high net worth individuals and they have all the problems that HNWIs also suffer from. 82% of physician's marriages will end in divorce. You already know that in a multi car pile up the attorneys will go after the richest guy with the best insurance regardless of fault. Why? It's not worth going after someone with no assets and insurance, even if they caused the accident – it just doesn't pay.

Your insurance company often has little incentive to protect you. They know that a court case is a crap shoot, and don't want to risk being lumbered with a telephone number verdict, so they'll settle. If the insurance you purchased doesn't run to the amount of the settlement they'll look to you to fund the rest and then you're in trouble...

Isn't it odd that the amount of "pain and suffering" compensation always equals the amount of the doctor's malpractice insurance? The settlement or verdict will then go on your record. Good luck finding insurance, let alone a good price after that.

With all the problems we've just mentioned, the difficulty of finding insurance and sky rocketing premiums many physicians are being forced into, or deciding to go without insurance and are "going bare". If you do this it only makes sense to protect your assets in case the unthinkable happens.

Relax. You're about to learn a lot more about asset protection in the next few hours than most lawyers do. Protecting your assets will not only be de-mystified for you, you'll learn why it needs to be done and how to do it. You will also join the ranks of many businessmen and celebrities who are protected, but also tens of thousands of other physicians who have already taken steps to protect their families from potential financial ruin and now "Practice without fear".

Ok. Enough with the whining, let's get on with helping you lower your risk and protect yourself...

What to do

- Keep reading this book.
- Determine exactly what your assets are. Fill out the following financial statement. This will show you what you need to protect and get you started thinking about how you might do that.

Financial statement

Asset	Value	Amount owed against asset(mortgage or bank loan)	Net value
Real Estate owned			
Bank accounts			
Cars			
Boats			
Planes			
Stock portfolio			
Bond portfolio			
Annuities			
Mortgages owned			

Loans/notes due you			
Other passive income sources			
401K, IRAs, Retirement accounts			
Your practice including patient book, good will, equipment, receivables and real estate			
Jewelry			
Coins and other collectables			
Total value of artwork			
Furniture			
Hobby equipment			
Intellectual			

Property			
Patents			
Miscellaneous			
TOTAL			

You should also consider Inheritances(past or future)

Action points

- Determine who your heirs are or should be.
- Give your heirs anything you are not using, plan on using, haven't used for the last year or two or no longer want, e.g. vacation homes, furniture, art work. You can use either a deed of gift, a quitclaim, warranty deed or simple sale agreement for this.
  Be very careful who you trust your assets to as relationships may change.
- You can also "give" an asset to a charity, but retain the use, and income from it, for your lifetime(see charitable remainder trusts in the trusts chapter).

IMPORTANT NOTE ON YOUR BORROWING ABILITY

If you give away all of your assets it may drastically reduce your ability to borrow money(take out mortgages, etc). Whilst doctors will probably not suffer as much as other professions due to our high incomes this is something that is worth bearing in mind.

When you place an asset in a different name taking out a loan against it may become extremely difficult as you just became "non-conforming", even if you are willing to guarantee the loan personally. You may like to consider talking out the loan/mortgage in your own name then using a quit claim to transfer the asset.

IMPORTANT NOTE ON LEGAL FORMS
INCLUDED IN THIS BOOK

All of the legal forms included here are believed to be correct, current and legal at the time of writing. You should seek appropriately qualified counsel to assist you in any type of estate planning or asset transfer. If you do not fully understand a form or is implications then you should not use it, or any other form for that matter. You make life and death decisions every day so this should be easy for you.

Resources

- Deed of gift – For giving an asset to someone or some thing.
- Quitclaim deed – For relinquishing your claim to an asset.
- Bill of sale – For selling an asset.
- General Warranty deed – Also for selling an asset.
- www.PracticeWithoutFear.com

Web resources

www.lectlaw.com
www.irlg.com
www.lawsmart.com

SAMPLE DEED OF GIFT FOR INTELLECTUAL PROPERTY

I, (name), the undersigned, of (address: street, city, state), being the artist and absolute owner of the following work: (title, description of work), do hereby transfer and assign all rights, title and interest of said work to (name of recipient) of (address: street, city, state), absolutely and forever. It is my intention that this transfer shall constitute a gift by me to (name of recipient).

Signed this ______ day of (month), (year)

____

(Signature) NAME OF ARTIST

Sworn to and Subscribed before me
this _______ day of (month), (year)

____

NOTARY PUBLIC

SAMPLE QUITCLAIM DEED

THIS QUITCLAIM DEED, Executed this ____ day of __________________, 20____, by first party

____

whose post office address is

____

to second party,

____

whose post office address is

____

WITNESSETH, That the said first party, for good consideration and for the sum of $_______________ paid by the said second party, the receipt whereof is hereby acknowledged, does hereby remise, release and quitclaim unto the said second party forever, all the right, title, interest and claim which the said first party has in and to the following described parcel of land, and improvements and appurtenances thereto in the County of______________________, State of_______________, to wit:

IN WITNESS WHEREOF, The said first party has signed and sealed these presents the day
and year first above written.

Signed, sealed and delivered in presence of:

____

Witness ________________________________ First Party

____

Witness ________________________________ Second Party

STATE OF }
COUNTY OF }

On________________________________before
me,__________________________, personally appeared
____,
personally known to me (or proved to me on the basis of satisfactory evidence) to be the person(s) whose name(s) is/are subscribed to the within instrument and acknowledged to me that he/she/they executed the same in his/her/their authorized capacity(ies), and that by his/her/their signature(s) on the instrument the person(s), or the entity upon behalf of which the person(s) acted, executed the instrument.

WITNESS my hand and official seal.

Signature______________________________

Affiant____Known____Unknown_____
ID Produced______________________
(Seal)

SAMPLE BILL OF SALE OF BUSINESS

For good and sufficient consideration, receipt of which is hereby acknowledged, the undersigned ("Seller") hereby sells, transfers and conveys to ("Buyer"):

1. All and singular, the goods and chattels, property and effects, listed in Schedule "A" annexed hereto, which is incorporated herein and made a part hereof; and

2. The whole of the good will of the ______________ business formerly operated by the undersigned which is the subject of this sale.

The undersigned warrants that said goods and chattels are free and clear of all encumbrances, that it has full right and title to sell the same, and that it will warrant and defend the same against the claims and demands of all persons.

The undersigned hereby warrants and covenants that I shall not within _______ years of the date of this instrument engage in the business of ________________ within __________________.

Dated:

______________________________ ______________________________

Witness (Seller)

SAMPLE GENERAL WARRANTY DEED

__________________, husband and wife, of __________, County, for valuable consideration, grant(s) with general warranty covenants, to ______________, husband and wife, for their joint lives, remainder to the survivor of them, whose tax mailing address is ______________ ___________________, the following REAL PROPERTY: Situated in the County of ___________, in the State of Ohio and in the Township of ___________:

Subject to conditions, restrictions, easements of record, and taxes, if any, now a lien.

Prior instrument reference: Volume ____, Page ____, Record of ________ of ___________, County, Ohio. ___________________ wife (husband) of the Grantor releases all rights of dower therein. Witness their hand this ______ day of _______, 1994.

Signed and acknowledged in presence of:

____

________________________________ ________________________________

Witness

____

________________________________ ________________________________

Witness

STATE OF OHIO;

COUNTY OF ______________; SS:

BE IT REMEMBERED, that on this ______ day of _______, 1997, before me, the subscriber, a Notary Public in and for said county, personally came ____________, the Grantors in the foregoing Deed, and acknowledged the signing thereof to be their voluntary act and deed.

IN TESTIMONY THEREOF, I have hereunto subscribed my name and affixed my seal on this day and year aforesaid.

________________________________Notary Public

Summary

- Lawyers are out to get you.
- You will be sued in your lifetime
- You stand a good chance of losing, regardless of fault.
- You could lose everything(in your name).

2. Lowering your medical risk

Getting sued isn't a pleasant experience regardless of how well your assets are hidden or protected. It takes time, money and aggravation to fight. Even though I will admit to gaining some perverse pleasure in giving some shyster lawyer the shaft no law suit has ever been a pleasant experience and you are always best off avoiding one in the first place. This chapter has a number of ways to help you do this.

Screening patients

Let's face it, getting sued by a patient is your number one fear. You always do your best to give a patient the very best care and advice that you possibly can. Sometimes, however things don't go as planned. It may be your fault, more likely there was very little you could do, a "perfect" result was unlikely or difficult to achieve or you just get a patient who isn't happy whatever you do. You don't HAVE to take someone on if you think they present an undue litigation risk. How do you spot these people? Complete the following check list:

Patient liability screening check list

- ✓ Ask them on their new patient information form – Have you ever been involved in legal action against a physician, or health organization(including a class action dispute).
- ✓ Call their previous providers, ask if the patient was a complainer, threatened to sue, or caused them any trouble.
- ✓ Ask the patient why they left their previous provider, or were referred to you.
- ✓ Go over past medical history with them and ask if they were happy with the results. If you hear a lot of complaining or negativity about past physicians you may like to dig a little deeper, or think twice before taking them on as a patient.
- ✓ Trust your 6th sense, it's usually right. Does the patient give you "the creeps" or make you feel uneasy.
- ✓ Does the patient appear too eager for treatment.
- ✓ Do they want copies of their records on their first visit?
- ✓ Do they have a relative or companion with them, even when it is unnecessary.
- ✓ Do they bring in old records that look like they've been photocopied a hundred times(they probably have).
- ✓ Explain any risks, have them sign with a witness.
- ✓ Won't sign a consent form.
- ✓ Wants treatment immediately for a disease they have had for a long time.
- ✓ Uses medical terminology when they are not involved in our field.
- ✓ Reeks of "compensationitis"
- ✓ Really bad mouths other physicians(they're going to do the same to you).
- ✓ Name dropping of friends or relations in the legal or community.
- ✓ Insists that you're their last hope to cure their problem(ego building but deadly).
- ✓ Unrealistic expectations in light of your specialty.
- ✓ The lady who insists you don't need a chaperone "with her" and who usually has seductive behavior or dress.

Make these checks a matter of practice, it's the patient who you failed to check who will end up causing you the problems.

(Form follows)

Patient liability screening check list

Check item	Points if applicable	Total
Involved in past legal action	10	
Previous provider problem	5	
Negative review of past M.D.	5	
Unhappiness with past results	3	
6th Sense	10	
Too eager for treatment	5	
Copies of records on 1st visit	10	
Friend or relative with them	2	
Much photocopied old records	10	
Medical terminology	5	
Won't sign consent form	10	
Wants immediate treatment for longstanding condition	10	
Reeks of "compensationitis"	10	
Name dropping of legal contacts	5	
Insists you're the "last hope"	10	
Unrealistic expectations	5	
No chaperone	10	
Threatened to sue previous doctor	10	
They have sought legal advice about their current condition	10	

Scoring

Score	**Action**
Score of 30 or less	Think carefully before accepting this person as a patient
Tick in *any* box that scores a 10	Think very seriously about accepting this person as a patient
Score of 50 or above	You are setting yourself up for a lawsuit by accepting this person as a patient
Score of 70 or above or ticks in any two boxes that score a ten	You should think seriously about giving them your standard notice as required by law.

Explaining risk, get them to sign
Be up front with a patient. Tell them that every procedure involves risk, some things may not be apparent that may have a bearing on the outcome of a treatment or procedure. Let them know the things that they can do to help themselves improve their health and show them that the outcome of their treatment is not entirely on your shoulders, but also rests with them. Document this and have their signature witnessed.

Show them that you are a professional who will do your utmost to ensure their safety, health and happiness. Make them an ally and a partner in their treatment. Listen to the patient and *really* listen. Patients don't care what you know unless they think that *you* care about *them*.

Waivers
Explain the malpractice situation to them, how bad it is, and why you need to protect yourself. Tell them that you can't afford to take on a new patient who may present a risk of suing. Explain that other doctors are in the same position and that if the patient brings a legal action against you that other doctors may be reluctant to treat them.

Make them sign the heftiest waiver you can(see resource section) to help protect you in the event of a law suit. Be aware though that no document can protect you fully and that no one can sign away their right to sue in the event of gross negligence. This is simply an extra level of protection to make someone think twice before suing and to help protect you in the event they do. If you are a surgeon you can get them to sign an agreement binding them to arbitration in the event of any dispute.

Everything you do procedurally to a patient needs to have a consent form signed by the patient and witnessed.

Second opinions
Get second opinions often. A concurring professional endorsing your judgment shows that at the time of a medical decision the course of action you undertook was deemed to be clear and right.

Your stationery

THIS IS IMPORTANT – MAKE SURE YOU READ IT

My notepads are all entitled "Private and confidential – Without Prejudice – Not for publication". If any of my notes fall into the wrong hands they can't publish it, or use it in any court case against me where it may prejudice my interests – of course I can waive this if I wish to use a note in my defense.

I also have a stamp made up with the above also noted. I use this to stamp everything I sign or write on. This makes it near impossible to put any kind of document or paper trail together that can be used in a court of law, any written evidence against you will be slim at best.

ANOTHER IMPORTANT POINT

Though documents with these titling cannot be used against you in a court of law the information in them still can be and can provide a useful jumping off point for further investigation. Do not take this as a free rein to write copious notes on whatever you want, this just provides an extra level of security for you.

Physician/patient arbitration agreement

This is an important document that you MUST have signed by each and every patient. It should be drawn up by a competent attorney and directly tailored to your sub-specialty. Some points that are well worth including are:

- Choose the law of a state other than that which you are registered in, Delaware is a good choice. This has the advantage of being swift and protective. It is also confusing for the suing patient and their attorney.
- You should state that the arbitration is binding at your behest only and that the alternative is $500 in full and final settlement(upon terms and conditions set out in your service agreement).
- They may take no action without first notifying you and receiving a copy of your customer service and dispute resolution document.

If it's good enough for Enron...
Fortune 10 corporations do it, lawyers and politicians do it, you can too...

Get yourself a shredder and make sure anything that you don't absolutely need gets shredded, you never know when something innocuous can bite you – besides you should be doing this anyway to protect your patients details.

Get a good shredder, at least one that cross cuts. It's worth looking for the type that governments use that turns paper to dust, it's a little more expensive, but worth the money. Any Private Investigator going through your trash is going to realize you are extremely committed to you privacy and finding anything that can be used against you will be extremely difficult.

The patient's chart is a legal document that cannot be destroyed, or altered in any way, shape or form and must be kept for 7 years. However, your personal notes are yours to do what you please with.

Email too
Never write anything that you wouldn't mind seeing published – email is not secure. You can, however encrypt any confidential information using a free program called Pretty Good Privacy – www.pgp.com. Two versions of this exist depending on whether you are a US citizen or not. The US one can be cracked, the International version is considered weapons grade and shouldn't be downloaded by any US citizen as it apparently cannot be compromised. Make sure you download the right one…

You saw it on Mission Impossible – "This message will self destruct". Your email can do this too with new software that will erase it after a certain set period of time. To delete a file on your computer is not secure enough as this data can easily be recovered by your teenage boy and other computer experts. A wide variety of software to permanently erase data is available at www.download.com .

Sexual harassment

Keep your hands off the interns, nurses and other cute hospital staff.

"Never shit where you eat" – Old Cuban saying

If you are a male physician never examine a female patient without a chaperone!.... NEVER

You may like to consider the following points when dealing with any female employee or colleague:

- If any of your female staff approaches you to have sex and you have it in your office that is sexual harassment even though you did not initiate it. This is not considered consensual sex.
- If you have sex with any employee at any time this is sexual harassment.
- Do not make sexual remarks, even jokingly, to any female employee.
- Do not touch a female staff member in any way that could be considered sexual.
- Do not tell sexual jokes around female employees.
- Do not stare at female staff's "anatomy"
- Do not leave pornography in your office, or on your computer.
- If a staff member is married and falls in love with you(with or without your knowledge) you may be liable for an "alienation of affection" law suit by their spouse.
- You will be spending more of your waking time with a female co-worker than your spouse, so be very careful of any developing emotional attachments and make sure to cut them off before they sprout.
- If you have doubts about a female staff member do not work late with her alone.
- Do not give preferential treatment to any female staff member.
- Keep any marital discord that you may be having out of the office.
- If you are a surgeon do not change into scrubs in front of a nurse(and vice versa).

(See section on Divorce)

You should also be aware that much of the above can also apply to persons of the same sex and can also apply to you if you are female.

Going Bare

The main thing that doctors are sued for is their malpractice insurance coverage. Doctors without malpractice insurance tend to be sued less(funny eh?). It's just not really worth it for the lawyers to "kick an empty bucket".

Your malpractice insurance is supposed to protect you from claims and you should think seriously before giving it up. If you decide to you may have to post a bond($250K here in Florida) with your state Department of Professional Regulation. Some states do not allow going bare at all. You may have to put this money up in cash, a pledge, or bond(which you can often buy for 10% of its face value) will often suffice.

Some hospitals may require you to have insurance to be attending there, so check before you drop your coverage. The situation varies from location to location, for example, a urologist in Brandon requires insurance to be attending whilst we know of OB/GYNs in Miami that do not. They were offered a $140K premium for $250K of coverage, so decided going bare made sense for them. Before taking this step you should obviously secure your assets, check with any medical institutions you deal with and your state licensing board(listed in the appendix at the back of the book).

You will also need to post notices that you are practicing without insurance and have patients sign a waiver procedure form prior to each encounter. Other variables that come in to play regarding going bare are

- Are you a full, or part time physician?
- Are you a hospital, or practice based physician?
- Do you do invasive, or non-invasive procedures?
- Do you see less than 10 patients a day, or more than 30?
- Do you have a problematic tail?
- Do you have a better, protected, economic use than the money you would save from your premiums? Visit www.tcalc.com for a number of tools that can help you calculate the alternative uses for your money.

All these issues will have a bearing from state to state.

Loan against accounts receivable

Most doctors have a high level of due billings. Lawyers know this and will calculate your historical net income from this and go after it. If you take a loan against your accounts receivable and invest this money in an asset protected form(e.g. an annuity), then this makes it less worth while for the attorney to pursue as they won't want to kick an empty bucket and will have to go up against the bank who is the first lien holder.

Change your specialty

Some specialties are more susceptible to law suits and large verdicts than others. Neurosurgeon is number one, if you're one, or are training to become one you may like to consider changing specialty. Obstetrics is number two, if you're an OB/GYN you may wish to become just a GYN.

Change your employer

Some hospitals, especially government facilities enjoy "sovereign immunity", i.e. they can't be sued. An "Eleemosynary" institution provides services to the poor for free and cannot be sued. Some of them will extend this immunity to you, or provide you with additional coverage if you provide some services to them.

Change your job

You may decide that being a doctor just isn't worth the aggravation any more. If you're about to retire, or young enough to do something else you may just want to quit and go consulting or retire. Other jobs you might be able to do with your training that have less liability and could pay better are:

- Congressman or senator – go Dr Frist
- University president
- Professional consultant to insurance companies
- "Professional witness" or consultant to law firms(go to the dark side).

Point of patient contact

"60 seconds to safety"™

When the patient is checking out and is satisfied is a great time to get in writing that this is the case, it will help you enormously is there is any future claim. Have them fill out and sign a quality control questionnaire and have the nurse witness it. If they balk about not having the time to do this say that their healthcare plan may need paperwork like this to prove that the procedures were carried out. By doing this you can be proactive in reducing your liability.

Having a patient fill out a form like this has several benefits:

- Lowers your liability in the event of a claim.
- Proof of excellent service
- Quality control
- Another layer of liability reduction

Mail a copy to every one of your past patients and offer a prize drawing for every returned copy. This will significantly help reduce the liability of your "tail", will provide you valuable feedback on how to deliver better patient service and will put your name in front of patients showing that you are an excellent physician who takes an active role in patient welfare – a great form of advertising.

Without Prejudice – Private and Confidential – Not for Publication

Sample Patient satisfaction questionnaire

Name:______________________________

Seen by Dr _______________

Physician assistant or nurse practitioner:

____

Date and time:______________________

Location of office:_______________________________

Procedure / Contact visit / Consultation (Delete as appropriate)

Were you seen in a timely manner?	Yes/No
Did the doctor address your health concerns?	Yes/No
Was the procedure performed satisfactorily?	Yes/No
Did the doctor adequately diagnose your problem?	Yes/No
Did the doctor listen to your concerns?	Yes/No
Did the doctor explain your problem to you?	Yes/No
Are you satisfied with this office visit?	Yes/No
Do you understand the recommendations made to you?	Yes/No
Are you willing to follow the prescribed recommendations?	Yes/No
Are you happy with your results?	Yes/No
Were the risks explained to you?	Yes/No
Were you told what results to expect from this procedure?	Yes/No
Was there a chaperone present during the exam?	Yes/No
Would you recommend the doctor to a friend?	Yes/No

Signed:

____

Patient

Date

Signed:

____

Nurse

Date

Good FORM is good business

A happy patient is a patient that stays away from the malpractice attorney. The happy patient likes you and knows you have their best interests at heart. How do you achieve this? Talk to them like they're one of your friends and take notes on their responses so that you can "remember" to ask them next time you see them. Always follow...

Family(enquire and learn what's going on)

Occupation(what do they do, how is it going?)

Recreation(how was their last golf game?, etc)

Message(and how are *YOU* doing?)

It takes less than two minutes to FORM every patient, and this should be done on every visit.

Action points

- ✓ Screen your patients
- ✓ Think about your profession
- ✓ Mark all your notes and correspondence appropriately
- ✓ Shred everything

Resources

- Get a new job, sell your practice, or buy one in a friendlier legal jurisdiction at:
- www.FreemanChase.com , a specialist medical search firm.
- Indemnity agreement – for indemnifying you from action
- Physician Patient arbitration agreement – for binding the patient to arbitration in the event of a dispute
- Sample letter to patients re going bare
- www.PracticeWithoutFear.com

SAMPLE INDEMNITY AGREEMENT

For the sum of $1.00 and other good and sufficient consideration, the receipt of which is hereby expressly acknowledged,

____, the first party and

____, the second party, on behalf of themselves, their heirs, assigns and successors, jointly and severally enter into this Indemnity Agreement to hold each other harmless form any suit, liability, claim, action or loss arising out of the below described incident:

WHEREFORE, it is further agreed that:

The first party shall have the following rights and the second party shall have the following duties:

The right to be adequately and reasonably defended by the second party should any claim arise regarding the before mentioned subject matter;

The right to defend his/herself should the second party fail to provide an adequate and reasonable defense and the right to seek compensation for the same from the second party;

The right to settle any action, suit, or claim, should the second party fail to defend the first party, and;

The right to bring an action or suit to seek recompensation for all reasonable attorney's and expenses required to enforce this agreement;

WHEREAS, the second party shall have the following rights and the first party shall have the following duties:

The right to timely and reasonable notice of any suit, liability, claim, action or loss asserted against the first party;

The right to reasonable cooperation in defense of said suit, liability, claim, action or loss on the part of the first party;

The right to settle any suit, liability, claim, action or loss so long as the settlement does not leave the first party exposed for any damage, claim, loss, or suit.

SO AGREED, to this ___ day of _________, 20__ .

____
First Party

____
Second Party

SAMPLE PHYSICIAN-PATIENT ARBITRATION AGREEMENT

Article1:

Agreement to Arbitrate:

It is understood that any dispute as to medical malpractice, that is as to whether any medical services rendered under this contract were unnecessary or unauthorized or were improperly, negligently, or incompetently rendered, will be determined by submission to arbitration as provided by State law, and not by a lawsuit or resort to court process except as State law provides for judicial review of arbitration proceedings. Both parties to this contract, by entering into it, are giving up their constitutional rights to have any such dispute decided in a court of law before a jury, and instead are accepting the use of arbitration.

Article 2:

All Claims Must be Arbitrated:

It is the intention of the parties that this agreement bind all parties whose claims may arise out of or relate to treatment or service provided by the physician including any spouse or heirs of the patient and any children, whether born or unborn at the time of the occurrence giving rise to any claim. In the case of any pregnant mother, the term "patient" herein shall mean both the mother and the mother's expected child or children. All claims for monetary damages exceeding the jurisdictional limit of the small claims court against the physician, and the physician's partners, associates, association, corporation or partnership, and the employees, agents and estates of any of them, must be arbitrated including, without limitation, claims for loss of consortium, wrongful death, emotional distress or punitive damages. Filing of any action in any court by the physician to collect any fee from the patient shall not waive the right to compel arbitration of any malpractice claim.

Article 3:

Procedures and Applicable Law:

A demand for arbitration must be communicated in writing to all parties. Each party shall select an arbitrator (party arbitrator) within thirty days and a third arbitrator (neutral arbitrator shall be selected by the arbitrators appointed by the parties within thirty days of a demand for a neutral arbitrator by either party. Each party to the arbitration shall pay such party's pro rata share of the expenses and fees of the neutral arbitrator, together with other expenses of the arbitration incurred or approved by the neutral arbitrator, not including counsel fees or witness fees, or other expenses incurred by a party for such party's own benefit. The parties agree that the arbitrators have the immunity of a judicial officer from civil liability when acting in the capacity of arbitrator under this contract. This immunity shall supplement, not supplant, any other applicable statutory or common law.

Either party shall have the absolute right to arbitrate separately the issues of liability and damages upon written request to the neutral arbitrator. The parties consent to the intervention and joinder in this arbitration of any person or entity which would otherwise be a proper additional party in a court action, and upon such intervention and joinder any existing court action against such additional person or entity shall be stayed pending arbitration. The parties agree that provisions of State law applicable to health care providers shall apply to disputes within this arbitration agreement, including, but not limited to, Code of Civil Procedure Sections 340.5 and 667.7 and Civil Code Sections 3333.1 and 3333.2. Any party may bring before the arbitrators a motion for summary judgment or summary adjudication in accordance with the Code of Civil Procedure. Discovery shall be conducted pursuant to Code of Civil Procedure section 1283.05, however, depositions may be taken without prior approval of the neutral arbitrator.

Article 4:
General Provisions:
All claims based upon the same incident, transaction or related circumstances shall be arbitrated in one proceeding. A claim shall be waived and forever barred if (1) on the date notice thereof is received, the claim, if asserted in a civil action, would be barred by the applicable California statute of limitations, or (2) the claimant fails to pursue the arbitration claim in accordance with the procedures prescribed herein with reasonable diligence. With respect to any matter not herein expressly provided for, the arbitrators shall be governed by the California Code of Civil Procedure provisions relating to arbitration.

Article 5:
Revocation:
This agreement may be revoked by written notice delivered to the physician within 30 days of signature. It is the intent of this agreement to apply to all medical services rendered any time for any condition.

Article 6:
Retroactive Effect:
If patient intends this agreement to cover services rendered before the date it is signed (including, but not limited to, emergency treatment) patient should initial below:
Effective as of the date of the first medical services
SAMPLE Patient's or Patient Representative's Initials
If any provision of this arbitration agreement is held invalid or unenforceable, the remaining provisions shall remain in full force and shall not be affected by the invalidity of any other provision.
I understand that I have the right to receive a copy of this arbitration agreement. By my signature below, I acknowledge that I have received a copy.
NOTICE: BY SIGNING THIS CONTRACT YOU ARE AGREEING TO HAVE ANY ISSUE OF MEDICAL MALPRACTICE. DECIDED BY NEUTRAL ARBITRATION AND YOU ARE GIVING UP YOUR RIGHT TO A JURY OR COURT TRIAL. SEE ARTICLE 1 OF THIS CONTRACT.
By:
SAMPLE
Patient's or Patient Representative's Signature
Date
By:
SAMPLE
Physician's or Authorized
Date
Representative's
Signature
By:
SAMPLE
Print
Patient's
Name
SAMPLE
SAMPLE
Print or Stamp Name of Physician,
(If Representative, Print Name and Relationship to Patient)
Medical Group or Association Name

A signed copy of this document is to be given to the Patient. Original is to be filed in Patient's medical records.

From the Florida Medical association:

SAMPLE: Letter to Patients

[First Name] [Last Name]
[Address 1]
[Address 2]
[City], [State], [Zip]

Dear [Title] [Last Name]:

You deserve the very best medical care. As your physician, I am dedicated to providing just that. Unfortunately, a serious healthcare crisis is facing our community that threatens my ability to provide you with the care you need.

Because Florida law doesn't do enough to stop frivolous lawsuits, doctors' insurance rates are skyrocketing out of control, forcing physicians to stop high-risk procedures, cut back on staff and new equipment, retire early or even move out of the state.

How will this affect you? Wait times are increasing at physicians' offices, and it is becoming harder to schedule immediate appointments with them -- when you most need medical care. Because many doctors can no longer afford new equipment, there is also a greater chance that health problems will not be diagnosed or treated as effectively. Worse yet, a doctor familiar with your history will no longer be available to you – leaving you to find one who can hopefully fit you into an already overloaded schedule.

Hospitals are being affected, too. With fewer doctors and specialists performing high-risk surgeries, emergency rooms are closing or forcing patients to wait longer for trauma care – when every second counts.

But we have an alternative. Many states, including California, have adopted legal reforms that limit excessive damages and hold down liability insurance costs for doctors and hospitals, while still fairly compensating patients with a legitimate case. A bill in Congress, H.R. 4600 and S. 2793, the HEALTH Act of 2002, would provide this for all Americans by protecting us from frivolous lawsuits and ensuring that we continue to receive the best healthcare in the world.

How can you help?

- Contact the congressional members below and express your support for the HEALTH Act of 2002.

U.S. Senator Bob Graham
524 Hart Senate Office Building
Washington, D.C. 20510
Phone (202) 224-3041 -- TDD (202) 224-5621
Fax (202) 224-2237

U.S. Senator Bill Nelson
818 Hart Senate Office Building
Washington, DC 20510
Phone: (202) 224-5274
Fax: (202) 228-2183

- Contact me for more information about the future of your healthcare.

- Spread the word among your family and friends.

Together, we can save Florida's healthcare system today -- and protect your health tomorrow.

Sincerely,
[Doctor]

3. Lowering your non-medical risk

The average American will be sued 5 times in their lifetime. The AVERAGE American. You are NOT an AVERAGE American. You have considerably greater intelligence, education and most of all MONEY. You stand a considerably higher chance, and the risk doesn't all come from your practice. There are numerous other areas that pose a significant risk to you that you probably haven't considered. We'll show you how to lower the risk now.

You should look into purchasing liability insurance and a good comprehensive umbrella insurance policy.

Children
Kids do stupid things, especially teenage kids. Nobody's are perfect and all will screw up in a big way at some point. Learning through failure is a necessary part of growing up. Paying for the mistake, and responsibility for it can often end up on your doorstep.

If your kids have others around to play and they're going to be doing any remotely dangerous activities, waterskiing, etc. Get them to have their parents sign a permission slip or waiver, they can list anything they don't want their kid doing on it. This may sound a bit anal and may annoy your child, but they're not the one who'll get sued when little Johnny decides to play with a snake he found in your garden…

A neighbor of ours got sued and had to pay about $50K out of pocket because a child's playmate had a non-serious accident whilst in their care. This kid still comes round to play, if I were in their shoes I'd kick his gluteus out and say "sorry your family is scum, so don't come round again". If you hear of any parents suing others over their child then don't let any of their children come round your house, or supervise them in any activity whatsoever.

Spouses

Unfortunately 82% of physician's marriages end in divorce. If two people's names are on a title then your potential for liability has just doubled and potential profit for you has just halved. Keep separate assets wherever possible. You can still look after your spouse's interests by listing them as a beneficiary on trusts etc. You need to get over the idea of having things in YOUR name and so do they. What matters is the control of the asset not having your name attached to it. If you are about to get married you should sign a prenuptial agreement. This is a touchy subject to bring up with your future spouse, so should be discussed in terms of an "estate plan".

ANOTHER IMPORTANT POINT

Your Pre-Marital agreement will be void if your spouse did not receive competent legal counsel, not recommended by you, a relative or associate. You must also disclose all your current assets at the time of signing. You should also be aware that this may be an acrimonious process with lawyers "running their clocks" on both sides. You should discuss as much as is possible with your future spouse before going to see the lawyers. If things get too fractious, then you should seriously consider why you are getting married in the first place.

D-I-V-O-R-C-E

"Hell hath no fury than the attorney of a woman scorned" – Shakespeare 2003

Though your soon to be ex-spouses' attorney may go after you with what appears to be a personal, bloody vendetta. Trust us, there is nothing personal about this for him. He couldn't care less about you personally, it's just business for him. The size of your assets and their control will determine how long the proceedings last. Divorces occur in "glacier time". If you are an established, successful, physician you can expect to spend one quarter of your entire assets on attorney's fees and it will typically last 2-4 years.

Women file for 80% of all divorces. The popular image of the wealthy doctor leaving his wife to run off with the busty, blonde nurse, leaving a wife to look after his kids is just that, an image, not reality. If you *think* you could be in trouble then protect yourself. The downside is that life will go on as normal, the upside is that your spouse may find further incentive to make your marriage work rather than leaving to find "something better".

You have a 3x greater chance of getting a divorce than a malpractice lawsuit. A divorce wipes out significantly more of your assets than a malpractice case, since those usually just go after the limit of your insurance coverage.

You might think that if you put all of your assets in both your name and your spouses that a lawyer won't be able to get any of your assets – possibly true if your estate is set up from the beginning that way. It has to be titled that way for 3 years or more to avoid the charge that the move was done to avoid a lawsuit.

This is asset protection for those that believe in the tooth fairy, Cinderella, Snow White and anyone else who believes the IRS loves you, politicians have your best interests at heart, all attorneys uphold the law and "no honey, I've never faked it."

Things you should think about before getting a divorce are:

1. Children
2. Marital home
3. Spousal contribution to your professional practice success – if he or she has ever worked in or on your practice be sure that they are properly compensated for their efforts or contributions. It's a lot cheaper to pay up front than out back.
4. Title to assets – if you don't own it you can't lose it.
5. Find the originals(copies are not as good) of all deeds, titles, or any other legal documents in your possession.
6. Don't go into a divorce thinking that you'll split up your assets and go your separate ways. As a physician your ability to significantly more than your spouse may be able to can cost you up to 90% of your assets.
7. Don't go into a divorce thinking that you'll do better in a trial than negotiating. Typically courts rule disproportionately in favor of one party than the other.
8. Don't go into a divorce with a solo attorney against a large law firm as the resources that can be brought against you are far more than a solo practitioner can deal with, especially if a case gets complex, as they have a tendency to do. Get yourself a large, "reputable"(oxymoron) law firm.
9. You may believe you know your spouse, in a divorce situation you will rapidly find out that this is not so.

Income for child support and alimony is based upon your last 2 yrs. If you are anticipating a lawsuit talk to your CPA about ways to reduce your income, e.g. deferments and pre-payment of debt.

Your past 2-3 yrs lifestyle may also be used against you in a divorce proceeding. You may like to re-consider expensive holidays and purchases if you are anticipating a lawsuit. What you don't own you can't lose, so get <u>everything</u> out of your name.

Protecting your 401K plan:

Give it away. Give it to a standard trust, they can then loan you the money back(you can even get a tax deduction on the interest you will pay on it). A charitable remainder trust will let you live off the income from it in your lifetime as long as the money is earmarked to go to a charity, which does not have to be specified, after your death.

Pets
This cute Labrador is called Sophie.

She lives with my wife and I, sleeps in our bed, we feed her, walk her, play with her and give her lots of attention. She's not "our" dog though, she's not "my" dog, she belongs to a Panamanian bearer share corporation with nominee directors. A little extreme? Absolutely not, here's why:

- A dog is an asset. Like any other asset it can be attached, seized and lost. It's unlikely a creditor would want your dog, but they might take it just to piss you off.
- A dog is a large source of potential liability. They run in front of cars, chew furniture, may intentionally, or unintentionally injure another animal, or human.

Not owning the dog removes it as a source of liability and an asset that can be lost. If the Panamanian nominee directors receive a letter fining them for allowing their dog to be off the leash I am sure they would give it due consideration before throwing it in the trash.

Our attorney also suggested that the dog may have "sought refuge" and that you are taking care of it on behalf of an absent owner. Of course this would only work if the dog is not registered to you and your name is not on any vet's bills, etc that are associated with the dog.

Asset protection should become a habit. When you acquire a new asset if losing it would be a concern to you then think carefully about how you title it.

If you open the front cover to this book you will see that we do not even own it. Copyright is an asset, so should be protected like any other.

Cars

This country has one of the easiest driving tests to pass in the First World. Every day I see at least 2 accidents on the interstate, the standard of driving is appalling. Add uninsured drivers and poorly kept vehicles into the mix and you have a recipe for disaster. If you're involved in an accident the other driver's attorneys will all say it's your fault when they find out you're a physician. If your family has four cars and they're in your name your potential liability just quadrupled.

If it's your son's car put it in his name, not yours. If he has an accident you're on the hook for it, not him, especially if he has no assets. If he owes you money for it, or you're worried about him selling it so he can run off with some girl or go do drugs then simply put a lien on it.

Have your child make the insurance and loan payments on the vehicle. Try to avoid signing as a guarantor on the loan as this may demonstrate liability and purchase a good umbrella policy.

Guarantees and endorsements

"A guarantor is a fool with a pen." – Dan Pena

Don't sign anything that isn't to do with you. Enough said.

If you have already guaranteed something or someone then have them release you and sign an indemnity.

Directorships

If it's not your company don't become a director, you can be held liable for anything that happens to them. If you must then have the corporation buy director's liability insurance for you and pay for your attorney fees. Please note that a director of a company can also be another corporation.

Volunteering

You do enough already, let someone else do it. We used to be protected by "good Samaritan" acts. Now lawyers will sue you for attempting to save someone if the outcome is not favorable.

Employees

The ideal company doesn't have any. "But I need X to answer my phone, and Y to be my nurse", I hear you say. Sure you do, and you can still have them. Tell them to set up a corporation, it will cost them less then $100. They can invoice you for their services, you don't have to pay their tax, health and liability insurance etc. It's a lot less cost and paperwork for you so you can afford to pay them more. They also get additional deductions, so everybody wins.

If they do something that generates a legal action then as they're not your employee you're not responsible, their company is. If you have four employees that you can turn into contractors then you've just eliminated four sources of liability.

While you're at it, there are no laws why you shouldn't be a contractor to your own practice. You get all the benefits listed above plus you've created an extra layer of legal protection for some scumbag lawyer to worm his way through.

Boards
As with directorships only sit on "advisory" boards unless you are getting well compensated and have a huge director's insurance plan in place.

Boats, jet skis, planes
These are all likely to crash, or be involved in incidents, especially if you charter them or let friends and family use them. Don't put them in your name. Put them in corporations then place liens against them(we'll show you how later). Also buy a good insurance policy for covering their use.

Neighborhood committees
Again here, our advice is let someone else do it. I sit on a committee, but the only reason I do is because the Home Owners Association was screwing with me and I pushed myself onto the committee to make sure they couldn't mess with me unnecessarily.

Political elections
Don't run for elections, or become a major spokesman(or woman) for anything. It singles you out to be a target for people that don't share your views.

Action points

- ✓ Remove all assets from your name
- ✓ Carefully examine your commitments and the risks they involve
- ✓ Screen your patients
- ✓ Think about your profession
- ✓ Mark all your notes and correspondence appropriately
- ✓ Shred everything

Resources

- Pre-nupital agreement – for signing prior to your marriage
- www.PracticeWithoutFear.com

SAMPLE PRE-MARITAL AGREEMENT (MUST BE APPROVED BY BOTH PARTIES ATTORNIES)

BE IT KNOWN,
this agreement is entered into on the day of , 20__ ,
between and .

Whereas, the parties contemplate legal marriage under the laws of the State of , and it is their mutual desire to enter into this agreement so that they will continue to own and control their own property, and are getting married because of their love for each other but do not desire that their present respective financial interests be changed by their marriage. Now, therefore, it is agreed as follows:

1. All property which belongs to each of the above parties shall be, and shall forever remain, their personal estate, including all interest, rents, and profits which may accrue from said property, and said property shall remain forever free of claim by the other.

2. The parties shall have at all times the full right and authority, in all respects the same as each would have it not married, to use, sell, enjoy, manage, gift and convey all property sd msy presently belong to him or her.

3. In the event of a separation or divorce, the parties shall have no right against each other by way of claims for support, alimony, maintenance, compensation or division of property existing of this date.

4. In the event of separation or divorce, marital property acquired after marriage shall nevertheless remain subject to division, either by agreement or judicial determination.

5. This agreement shall be binding and inure to the benefit of the parties, their successors, assigns and personal representatives.

This agreement shall be enforced with the laws of the State of .

Signed this day of , 20__ .

Witnessed:

____

Witness _______________________________ First Party

____

Witness _______________________________ Second Party

Summary

- There are many potential sources of risk
- What you don't own you can't lose
- There are many ways you can protect yourself from risk.

4.Isn't asset protection illegal?

No. It's never been illegal to protect your assets. It is illegal to attempt to protect or dispose of your assets to confound a creditor if you know you are going to be sued. It is perfectly legal to protect your assets, title them in any way you wish, sell them, mortgage them, or roll them up and smoke them as long as they belong to you, no one else has claim to them and you do so in good faith.

The concept of a trust as a non-living asset vehicle separate from an individual and surviving them after their death has been around since Roman times.

Celebrities routinely use trusts and corporations to protect their assets, it's perfectly acceptable and in the litigious society we live in makes perfect sense.

Does it work?
Even alleged murderer O.J. Simpson was able to use a trust to protect his assets from creditors and huge civil law suit penalties.

Is this guaranteed to work?

THIS IS IMPORTANT – MAKE SURE YOU READ IT

Nothing in life is 100% certain. You can buy the best trust from the best attorney, follow every law to the letter and still have a judge rule against you. Why? Because people make mistakes, people are prejudiced and people are lazy. Don't rely on someone else to defend you, it probably won't happen. How can you protect yourself adequately if nothing is certain?

Layering

You should use as many different layers of protection as you possibly can:

- Confuse and cloud the title to an asset as much as possible.
- Take as much equity out of an asset as you possibly can.
- Do everything in your power to make an asset worthless to someone else.

While you cannot be positive that one single protective measure can thwart an attack, the more layers you use to protect yourself the less worthwhile you are to sue and the more likely your opponent is to give up.

Does merely wearing a seatbelt protect you from dying in a car crash? No. What if you wore a seatbelt, drove safely, had a well maintained, large, car, with airbags? Your chances would be quite a bit higher wouldn't they? It's the same with asset protection – use everything at your disposal.

Summary:

- Asset protection is legal
- People have protected their assets legally for thousands of years
- Structures like trusts and corporations are used commonly everyday by people from all walks of life to protect themselves.

Further reading:
Bullet Proof Asset Protection – William S. Reed J.D.
The Sovereign Individual – Lord Rees Mogg
PT1 – W.G.Hill

Resources:
www.SoverignSociety.com
www.PracticeWithoutFear.com

5. What happens when you're sued

It all starts with someone being pissed off at you. You may have done something wrong, you may not – it's not really that relevant to the process, or even the outcome.
That person will go and see a lawyer. If it's a non-medical case, like a dispute with a neighbor the lawyer will ask for a retainer of $300 or so, if it's a malpractice the snake will wipe the drool from his mouth and offer to take the case on contingency for a share of the profits (up to 60%).

In a medical malpractice case, if it does not get arbitrated, the plaintiff's lawyer will always seek the maximum of your insurance. Even if you are a minor consultant in a multiple physician case you may well become the principal defendant if you have the deepest pockets.

Next he'll call a private investigator. For $150 or so your name will be run against more databases than you knew existed. He will go after your email, telephone records, mobile phone bills going back two years, court filings, credit card statements, bank accounts, etc. At the end of the afternoon the attorney will have the following information in their sweaty palms:

- Full name
- Address
- Telephone number

- Place of business
- Civil law records
- Criminal law records
- Social security number
- Immigration status
- Home, how much you paid
- Mortgage amount
- Aliases
- Family members(searches will be done on them too)
- Attorney
- Accountant
- Known associates
- Companies
- Directors
- News clippings
- Drivers license
- Vehicles
- Boats
- Aircraft
- Professional licenses
- Tax records
- Credit
- Associated addresses
- Physical description
- Past addresses
- Liens
- Registered quit claims
- Neighbors past and present with contact details
- Other people using associated addresses
- Military service
- Bankruptcies
- Judgments
- Sex offender databases
- Etc.

In short he'll know more about you than your spouse.

He'll call the client back into his office and show them the information, the client will be impressed. He will then place you in one of two categories:
A. You have assets worth going after.
B. You have no assets, or are deeply in debt.
You want him to place you in the second one.

"Ownership of assets indicates wealth"

This is a very good reason for not owning anything. Wealthy people can easily pay claims and have assets attached, paupers are seldom pursued. Since many of the affluent have already taken steps to protect their wealth, a rich and unprotected physician is a naïve and juicy target for the unscrupulous attorney.

If you're in the second category he'll advise the client he won't take the case on contingency, if the guy really has it out for you he'll take the case but he'll want $10K up front to cover time and expenses. Your file will then drop somewhere near the bottom of his pile while he wastes his clients money "running his clock" and indulging in various ineffective but time consuming procedures.

If you're in the first category you're in trouble...

You can then expect a nasty letter from the attorney followed by filings, attempts to settle and then maybe a messy court case.

You're only required to keep 7 years of records. Shred anything older. What you don't have and can't produce cannot be litigated over. Get rid of all unwanted pieces of paper. Never try to amend a record, it's too easy to get caught out by modern scientific methods of dating paper and ink.

You can't touch your assets to re-structure them once you have been sued, or in anticipation of a lawsuit, a judge can rule your re-structuring invalid.

Safety deposit boxes
Never use one in the same city as you or your practice. Safety deposit boxes are the bank's property, not yours. If the bank goes out of business you can lose everything. Always keep money in a non-bank safety deposit box.

Resources
www.PracticeWithoutFear.com

Summary

- A lawyer will only want to go after you in a contingency case if you have assets he can seize.

6. Corporations

You are well aware that a company can help limit your liability. If you own stock in General Electric and it gets sued you don't expect a lawyer to turn up on your doorstep. When you invest in a company it's assets become separate to yours and you cannot lose more than your total investment as your assets cannot be claimed by the company's creditors.

Your liability is limited and that's why you use a company to protect your assets, or perform any type of procedure through. A company is also a separate entity, i.e. it is not you. You, your companies and trusts are entirely separate and should be treated as such. If there's going to be a lawsuit each has to be sued separately. However, a physician and his personal medical corporation are not protected for professional liability, therefore they should have as few assets as possible.

The more different "pots" you have your assets in then the more different actions must be filed and proved for the asset to be lost. If you just use one then an accident with one car could cost you the use of all of them, plus your house, etc.

S versus C corps:
An S corporation is closely tied to your personal financial statement and this makes it more difficult to argue that it is separate from you. It may be useful if you are expecting large losses from the business venture, otherwise it is near useless in terms of protecting your identity.

LLCs:
You can set up an LLC and have it taxed as a "pass though partnership". This means that the company itself doesn't pay tax, the recipients of its profits do based upon their own tax rate. This means that you do not need to pay tax more than once and can have other benefits depending on how you structure it.

A limited liability company does not necessarily protect you – an attorney may try to "pierce the corporate veil", prove that the company is essentially you and acts in your interests.

Factors that must be proved to pierce the corporate veil:

- Fraud
- Misstatements in setting up the company
- Inadequate capitalization of the organization
- Failure to follow corporate formalities and procedures

  A failure to record proper minutes of corporate meetings constitutes a lack of corporate responsibility invalidating the corporation. Failure to keep documentation of proper minutes is the most common way in which doctors have their corporation protection nullified.
- Co-mingling of assets and money.
  - This is the second most common method of corporate nullification(please consult your C.P.A. to show you how to avoid this).
- Corporations used interchangeably.

Another good trick, one I like to use a lot to go after a director personally is this: You find some illegal action the company has carried out; read their memorandum and articles of incorporation – you will find out that these do not permit to the company officer to carry out the illegal act. This means that they carried out the act on their own accord, not that of the company, that means you can sue them personally.

While we're on the subject, always put the company's name under yours when sending any letter. If you don't it can be argued that you were using company stationary for your own personal use and they can go after you. That's a nice evil trick most people don't know about.

Nominee directors:

You do not have to be a listed director on your company. Many jurisdictions allow "nominee directors", people that allow their name to be listed on your company. If you can do this then use them. You will not show up on any director search and can be shown to have an, at best, tenuous relation to the corporation. Being "CEO" is not that impressive to anyone who knows titles are fairly meaningless in corporate America. I believe that representing the company using a fairly junior title implies that everyone "above" you in the company is of an even more superior quality than you and implies it is a very high quality organization.

You may wish to register outside your current jurisdiction to make sure that decisions regarding the entity cannot be taken at a local level. Offshore companies can also enjoy significant other benefits over an onshore company, see our offshore chapter for more information.

Action points

- Form a company if you don't already have one
- Close an S Corp if you have one and consider an LLC.
- Keep your corporate records up to date.
- Don't co-mingle funds.
- Form more companies to hold your assets and to work through.

Resources

www.uscorporations.com
www.apfpconsulting.com
www.PracticeWithoutFear.com

Summary

- A company is an excellent and relatively cheap way to protect your assets.
- Make sure you make and record annual meetings with minutes

7. Trusts

You can create a trust to hold your assets. Once you do this you don't own them anymore. This is an important point. If you don't own them they can't be taken from you. If the trust is "revocable" then the assets can however be seized. A revocable trust is, in my opinion, not worth the paper it is written on.

A trust can survive your death and since it isn't you is not liable for any death duties. A trust needs someone or something to give it assets for it to start. This is called a grantor. You can do this yourself, but just to make it harder to a creditor to try and pierce the corporate veil you should get someone else to do it, this gives an appearance of you being somewhat separated from the process. Have a relative or close family friend do this, failing that your trust former can pay someone to do this.

A trust can either be revocable or irrevocable. Some people feel uncomfortable with the idea of "giving" away "their" assets and so want a revocable trust. This is really dumb as it can be argued the assets haven't really left your possession. Make sure it's irrevocable.

How a trust is run depends on a document called the "letter of wishes". This explains how you wish the trust to be administered, e.g. It could be run for your benefit, but when you die for the benefit for your cat and a local animal shelter. If you are the sole beneficiary it could be argued that it is little more than a shield for you, so put some family members in there and a couple of charities. You can always change it later and your letter of wishes determines who gets what money, if any.

You can decide on the powers of the trustees to decide how the trust should be administered. It is important not to be a trustee yourself. Appoint an "independent" professional. Many jurisdictions also allow a "protector" who you can ask to step in and look after your interests should you disagree with a decision. You can also sue your trustees if they administer a trust contrary to the letter of wishes or the law.

You may wish to register outside your current jurisdiction to make sure that decisions regarding the entity cannot be taken at a local level.

A "Family living trust" is like giving all your assets to your children in advance. The trust is 99% owned by your children and 1% by you. It is however 1% controlled by your children and 99% controlled by you.

Ownership can pass to your children's grandchildren skipping a generation. This has tax advantages and also means that every generation of the family has a strong incentive to keep on good terms with each other. When you get older you will understand that younger relatives like to drop by to "visit the money". A trust like this is called "generation skipping".

A "charitable remainder trust" is where you may give your assets to the trust and live off the income from those assets for the remainder of your life as long as the money is earmarked to go to a charity upon your death. You do not have to specify a charity.

Other types of trust

Accumulation and Maintenance Trusts
Almost always established for the benefit of the settlor's children. The trust deed will specify that the trust funds are to be used for the education and maintenance of the children up to a certain age, at which point they are entitled to their share of the trust capital.

Asset Protection Trust
A trust that is established in a jurisdiction which has provisions in its trust legislation to provide enhanced protection for the assets of the trust fund.

Bare Trusts
In the case of a bare or 'simple' trust the trustee holds property for one or more beneficiaries absolutely and such beneficial owners may call for the trust property to be vested in them and the trustee must comply. The trustee has no powers over the property other than to hold it to the order of the beneficiary.

Discretionary Trust
A Trust where distribution of funds to the beneficiaries is mainly at the discretion of the Trustees.

Fixed Trust
A Trust where the interests of the beneficiaries are clearly defined

Hybrid Companies
These have the attraction of looking like companies but with many of the same features as a trust. A typical example would be a company limited by guarantee and having shares. These companies allow the shareholders to have voting and administrative powers, while the beneficial owners could be non-shareholder members in whom all the rights to income and capital are vested. Such a structure would separate the beneficial interest from the control. This arrangement has a number of benefits, one of which is that a company may be more readily accepted as an investing entity in some civil law countries than a trust would be.

Interest in Possession Trusts
These differ from discretionary trusts in that the settlor will normally be automatically entitled to the income and capital of the trust.

Inter-Vivos Trust
An expression used to indicate a Trust created during the Settlor's lifetime

Pension Funds
Pension fund are often held through a trust medium. Trusts offer the flexibility required to allow contributions for any number of employees to be invested together in a mutually beneficial manner and to allow payments to the employee or his family in any number of different circumstances. To this end, pension trusts tend to be purely discretionary.

Perpetuities
While private trusts are in almost all cases subject to restrictions on their lifetime and tend to be limited either to fixed periods between 80 and 125 years or by reference to lives in being, charity trusts may be drafted in such a way that they may continue indefinitely.

Precatory Trusts
A precatory trust may be construed either as an absolute gift to the 'trustee' with only a moral obligation on him to fulfil the donor's wishes or as a formal trust where the Courts may enforce the donor's requests.

Protective/Spendthrift or Alimentary Trusts
A US spendthrift trust, on the other hand, requires the trustees to pay the trust income to a beneficiary even after bankruptcy but prevents creditors having rights against the trust income or capital. Legislation has tended to restrict the amount of income which may be protected in such a way from the claims of creditors.

Purpose Trust
A purpose trust does not have beneficiaries and is established to achieve a specific purpose. The main uses of purpose trusts have been for charitable purposes and one-off projects such as commercial ventures.

Secret Trusts
Secret trusts arise where a Will or an inter-vivos disposition give no indication that the recipient is to hold the property received on trust. The action which converts the absolute gift to one creating a secret trust is the communication by the donor to the recipient of his intention that the property be held for another and the acceptance (either express or implied through silence) by the trustee of that role.

If you desire aspects from different types of trust you can usually have these drafted into the trust agreement. We wouldn't recommend you do this yourself, it's really an attorney's job, but it can be done. The terms above are basically descriptive of the features and purposes of the trusts.

Action points

- Form a trust

Resources

- Irrevocable trust agreement
- Charitable remainder trust agreement
- Sample letter of wishes
- www.PracticeWithoutFear.com

Trust formation agents
www.icsl.com

SAMPLE IRREVOCABLE TRUST AGREEMENT

IRREVOCABLE TRUST AGREEMENT made _______________, 19__, between

_______________________(the "Grantor"), and _______________ and ___________________(the "Trustees").

1. TRUST PROPERTY. The Grantor, desiring to create trusts for the benefit of his adult children and for other good and valuable consideration, irrevocably assigned to the Trustees of the property described in attached Schedule A (the "Trust Property"), in trust, for the purposes and on the conditions hereinafter stated.

2. DISPOSITIVE PROVISIONS. The Trustees shall hold the property for the primary benefit of

____,

and the Trustees shall hold, manage, and invest the trust property, and shall collect and receive the income, and after deducting all necessary expenses incident to the administration of the trusts, shall dispose of the corpus and income of the trusts as follows:

(a) The Trustees shall pay the entire net income of the trust, quarter annually, to the beneficiaries of the trust, provided that there shall be paid over absolutely to the beneficiaries at age _______ the corpus of the trust.

(b) If any of the beneficiaries shall die before attaining the age of ______ years, the trust for his or her benefit shall cease, and the corpus, together with any undistributed income, shall be paid over absolutely to the issue of the beneficiary then living per stirpes; but if there be no issue, then to the other beneficiaries if living, either outright, or, if the other beneficiary shall not have then attained the age of _____ years, in trust, to be added to, held, administered, and distributed as part of the trust for the other beneficiary; but if the other beneficiary is not then living, then absolutely to the then living issue of the other beneficiary per stirpes; and if there is no issue, then to the estate of the beneficiary for whom the trust was being held originally.

(c) Notwithstanding anything contained to the contrary, if at any time while the trusts are in force any financial emergency arises in the affairs of either of the primary beneficiaries of the trusts, or if the independent income of either of the beneficiaries (exclusive of the income from any trust created for his or her benefit by the Grantor) and all other means of support are insufficient for the support of the beneficiary, in the judgment of the Trustees, the Trustees shall pay over to the beneficiary, solely out of the corpus of the trust for his or her benefit, at any time and from time to time, the sum or sums as the Trustees shall deem necessary or appropriate in their discretion.

3. TRUSTEES' POWERS. In the administration of the trusts, the Trustees shall have the
following powers, all of which shall be exercised in the fiduciary capacity, primarily in the interest of the beneficiaries:
(a) To hold and continue to hold as an investment the property, of any additional property which may be received by them, so long as they deem proper, and to invest and reinvest in any securities or property, whether or not income-producing, deemed by them to be for the best interest of the trusts and the beneficiaries.
(b) To rent or lease any property of the trusts for the time and upon the terms and for the price or prices as in their discretion and judgment may seem just and proper and for the best interest of the trusts and the beneficiaries.
(c) To sell and convey any of the property of the trusts or any interest, or to exchange it for other property, for the price or prices and upon the terms as in their discretion
and judgment may be deemed for the best interest of the trusts and the beneficiaries.
(d) To make all repairs and improvements at any time deemed necessary and proper to and upon real property constituting a part of the trusts.
(e) To deduct, retain, expend, and pay out of any money belonging to the trusts any and all necessary and proper expenses in connection with the operation and conduct of the trusts.
(f) To vote upon all securities belonging to the trusts, and to become a party to any stockholders' agreements deemed advisable by them in connection with
the securities.
(g) To consent to the reorganization, consolidation, merger, liquidation, readjustment of, or other change in any corporation, company, or association.
(h) To compromise, settle, arbitrate, or defend any claim or demand in favor of or against the trusts.
(i) To incur and pay the ordinary and necessary expenses of administration, including (but not byway of limitation) reasonable attorneys' fees, accountants' fees, investment counsel fees, and the like.
(j) To act through an agent or attorney-in-fact, by and under power of attorney duly

executed by the Trustees, in carrying out any of the authorized powers and duties.

(k) To borrow money for any purposes of the trusts, or incidental to their administration, upon their bond or promissory note as trustees, and to secure their repayment by mortgaging, creating a security interest in, or pledging or otherwise encumbering any part or all of the property of the trusts.

(l) To lend money to any person or persons upon the terms and in the ways and with the security as they may deem advisable for the best interest of the trusts and the beneficiaries.

(m) To engage in business with the property of the trusts as sole proprietor, or as a general or limited partner, with all the powers customarily exercised by an individual so engaged in business, and to hold an undivided interest in any property as tenant in common or as tenant in partnership.

(n) To determine the manner in which the expenses incidental to or in connection with the administration of the trusts shall be apportioned as between corpus and income.

(o) The Trustees may freely act under all or any of the powers by this Agreement given to them in all matters concerning the trusts, after forming their judgment based upon all the circumstances of any particular situation as to the wisest and best course to pursue in the interest of the trusts and the beneficiaries, without the necessity of obtaining the consent or permission of any interested person, or the consent or approval of any court. The powers granted to the Trustees may be exercised in whole or in part, from time to time, and shall be deemed to be supplementary to and not exclusive of the general powers of trustees pursuant to law, and shall include all powers necessary to carry them into effect.

4. LIMITATION ON POWERS. Notwithstanding anything contained to the contrary, no powers enumerated or accorded to trustees generally pursuant to law shall be construed to enable the Grantor, or the Trustees or either of them, or any other person, to sell, purchase, exchange, or otherwise deal with or dispose of all or any parts of the corpus or income of the trusts for less than an adequate consideration in money or monies worth, or to enable the Grantor to borrow all or any part of the corpus or income of the trusts, directly or indirectly, without adequate interest or security.

5. CORPUS AND INCOME. The Trustees shall have the power to determine the allocation of receipts between corpus and income and to apportion extraordinary and share dividends between corpus and income.

6. TRUSTEES' AUTHORITY AND THIRD PARTIES. No person purchasing, renting, or leasing any of the property of the trusts, or in any manner dealing with the trusts or with the Trustees, shall be required to inquire into the authority of the Trustees to enter into any transaction, or to account for the application of any money paid to the Trustees on any account.

7. ADDITIONAL PROPERTY. The Grantor reserves the right to himself or to any other person at any time, by deed or will, to add to the corpus of either or both of the trusts, and any property added shall be held, administered, and distributed as part of the trust or trusts. The additional property shall be allocated between the trusts in accordance with any directions given in the instrument of transfer.

8. ACCOUNTING BY TRUSTEES. The Trustees may render an accounting at any time to the beneficiaries of the trust, and the written approval of a beneficiary shall be final, binding, and conclusive upon all persons then or thereafter interested in the trust for that beneficiary. The Trustees may at any time render a judicial account of their proceedings for either or both of the trusts.

9. COMPENSATION OF TRUSTEES. The Trustees waive the payment of any compensation for their services, but this waiver shall not apply to any successor trustee who qualifies and acts under this Agreement except that no person who adds to the corpus of either or both of the trusts shall ever be entitled to any compensation.

10. SUCCESSOR TRUSTEES. Either of Trustees shall have the power to appoint his or her successor Trustee. If either of the named Trustees shall die, resign, become incapacitated, or refuse to act further as Trustee, without having appointed a successor Trustee, the other named Trustee may, but shall not be required to, appoint a successor Trustee. The appointment of a successor Trustee shall be made by a duly acknowledged instrument delivered to the primary beneficiaries and to the person, if any, then acting as Trustee.

11. BOND AND LIABILITY OF TRUSTEES. Neither of the two (2) named Trustees shall be required to give any bond or other security. The Trustees shall not be liable for any mistake or error of judgment in the administration of the trusts, except for willful misconduct, so long as they continue to

exercise their duties and powers in a fiduciary capacity primarily in the interests of the beneficiaries.

12. IRREVOCABILITY. The trusts shall be irrevocable, and the Grantor expressly waives all rights and powers, whether alone or in conjunction with others, and regardless of when or from what source he may have acquired such rights or powers, to alter, amend, revoke, or terminate the trusts, or any of the terms of this Agreement, in whole or in part. By this instrument the Grantor relinquishes absolutely and forever all his possession or enjoyment of, or right to the income from, the trust property, and all his right and power, whether alone or in conjunction with others, to designate the persons who shall possess or enjoy the trust property, or the income.

13. SITUS. This trust has been executed and delivered in the State of ______________ and shall be construed and administered according to the laws of that state. In witness whereof the Grantor and the Trustees have executed this Agreement in ________________.

____

Grantor: [NAME]

____

Trustee: [NAME]

SAMPLE THE JOHN DOE
CHARITABLE REMAINDER ANNUITY TRUST

THIS TRUST AGREEMENT (hereinafter "this Agreement"), made as of the ______ day of ______________, 2003, between **JOHN DOE** of New Castle, Delaware,
as Donor and **AMERICAN GUARANTY & TRUST COMPANY**, a Delaware corporation, as Trustee. The Donor, desiring to establish The **JOHN DOE CHARITABLE REMAINDER ANNUITY TRUST**, a charitable remainder annuity trust within the meaning of Rev. Proc. 90-32 issued by the Internal Revenue Service and Section 664 (d)(1) of the Code, do hereby deliver to the Trustee, and the Trustee acknowledges receipt of, the property described in Schedule A hereto annexed. The Trustee agrees to hold said property in trust for the uses and purposes, and subject to the terms and conditions, hereinafter set forth.

ARTICLE I - DEFINITIONS

In this Agreement the following terms (in quotations) shall have the meanings set
forth next to them:

A. "Donor" - **JOHN DOE.**

B. "Recipient" - a person entitled to receive a payment under Article II below.

C. "Trustee" - the trustee then serving in said office. The initial trustee is American Guaranty & Trust Company.

D. "Executor" - the one or more executors, administrators or personal representatives of an estate, including an executor of either gender.

E. "Legal representative" - (1) the one or more legally appointed guardians, conservators or similar legal representatives then serving, (2) an attorney-in-fact if the power of attorney appointing such attorney authorizes such attorney to exercise a right conferred hereunder or (3) the parent of a minor to the extent that the laws of the state in which the minor resides, without requiring a judicial proceeding, give the parent powers substantially equivalent to those of a guardian, conservator or the like over the property of the minor. If a person has more than one of the aforesaid types of legal representative at the time, the act of a representative under clause (1), if there is one, shall be binding, and, if there is none, the act of a representative under clause (2) shall be binding.

F. "Fund" - an open-end mutual fund or its successor of which AMERICAN

GUARANTY & TRUST COMPANY, of Newark, Delaware ("AG&T") or any affiliate thereof is investment advisor, including without limitation each of the Sentinel Funds.
G. "Code" - the Internal Revenue Code of 1986 as currently in force and the comparable provisions of later laws.
H. "Trust income" - the income of the trust as defined in Section 643(b) of the Code and the regulations promulgated thereunder, taking into account the items properly chargeable thereto, including without limitation the expenses of administering the trust.

ARTICLE II - DISTRIBUTIONS
A. In each taxable year of the trust during the Donor's lifetime, the Trustee shall pay to the Donor an annuity amount equal to **SEVEN percent (7%)** of the net fair market value of the trust assets as of the date hereof. The annuity amount shall be paid in equal quarterly installments at the end of each March, June, September and December from income and, to the extent that income is not sufficient, from principal. At least as often as annually, any income of the trust for a taxable year in excess of the annuity amount shall be added to principal. If the net fair market value of the trust assets is incorrectly determined, then within a reasonable period after the final determination of the correct value for federal tax purposes, the Trustee shall pay to the Recipient (or the Recipient's executor), in the case of an undervaluation, or shall receive from the Recipient (or the Recipient's executor), in the case of an overvaluation, an amount equal to the difference between the annuity amounts properly payable and the annuity amounts actually paid. The Trustee shall prorate the annuity amount on a daily basis for a short taxable year. The obligation of the Trustee to pay the annuity amount shall terminate with the regular quarterly payment next preceding the death of the Recipient.

B. Upon the death of the Recipient, the Trustee shall distribute all of the then principal and income of the trust, other than any amount due the Recipient or the Recipient's estate under the above provisions, to the following charitable organizations or their successors (each hereinafter referred to as a "Charitable Organization") to be used for the Charitable Organizations' general purposes, in the amounts or percentages or proportions thereof set forth next to each Charitable Organization's name:
One Hundred Percent (100%) to : THE AMERICAN GIFT FUND
220 Continental Drive, Suite 401
Newark, Delaware, 19713

If any Charitable Organization is not an organization described in each of Sections 170(b)(1)(A), 170(c), 2055(a) and 2522(a) of the Code at the time when any principal or income of the trust is to be distributed to it, the Trustee shall distribute such principal or income to such one or more organizations then described in each of Sections 170(b)(1)(A), 170(c), 2055(a) and 2522(a) of the Code and in such amounts and proportions as the Trustee shall determine in its sole discretion.

ARTICLE III - GENERAL ANNUITY TRUST PROVISIONS

A. No additional contributions shall be made to the trust after the initial contribution.

B. The Trustee shall make distributions at such times and in such manner as not to subject the trust to tax under Section 4942 of the Code. Except for the payment of the annuity amount to the Recipients, the Trustee is prohibited from engaging in any act of self-dealing as defined in Section 4941(d) of the Code, from retaining any excess business holdings as defined in section 4943(c) of the Code which would subject the trust to tax under Section 4943 of the Code, from making any investments which would jeopardize the charitable purpose of the trust within the meaning of Section 4944 of the Code and shall not make any taxable expenditures as defined in Section 4945(d) of the Code.

C. In creating this trust, the Donor intends to obtain the full benefit of any income, gift and estate tax charitable contribution deductions to which Donor (and Donor's estate) may be entitled under the Code, and for the trust to qualify as a charitable remainder annuity trust under Section 664 of the Code and the regulations promulgated thereunder. Accordingly, the trust shall be interpreted, valued, managed, invested, administered and governed in a manner consistent with the Donor's intent.

D. No part of any federal estate tax or state estate or other tax imposed by reason of the death of the Donor or a Recipient, any debt of the Donor's or Recipient's estate, funeral expense of the Donor or Recipient or expense of administering the estate of a Donor or Recipient shall be paid from the property of this trust. Unless the Donor shall have made other provisions for the payment of said taxes and expenses, any such taxes and expenses shall be paid (or reimbursed) by the person (or the estate of such person) upon or to whose beneficial interest such taxes and expenses were imposed or charged such taxes.

E. The trust created hereunder is irrevocable and may not be amended except that:

1. The Trustee shall have the power, acting alone, to amend the trust in writing at any time or times in any manner required for the sole purpose of insuring that the trust hereunder qualifies and continues to qualify as a charitable remainder annuity trust within the meaning of Section 664(d)(1) of the Code.
2. The Donor shall have the right, exercisable from time to time in writing or writings signed by the Donor and delivered to the Trustee the Donor is living, but not by will, to change the Charitable Organizations listed in Article II, Paragraph B to such one or more other Charitable Organizations as are described in Sections 170(b)(1)(A), 170(c), 2055(a) and 2522(a) of the Code, and to change the amounts, percentages and or proportions of the trust property to be held for or distributed to such organizations.

ARTICLE IV - INVESTMENTS
A. No provision of this trust shall be construed to restrict the Trustee from investing the trust assets in a manner which could result in the annual realization of a reasonable amount of income or gain from the sale or disposition of trust assets. In this instrument, "reasonable return" means the annual realization of such reasonable amount of income or gain.
B. While the Donor is living, the Donor shall have the right from time to time by a writing delivered to the Trustee and to each person appointed and removed to appoint and remove one or more investment advisers to have the power and authority in their uncontrolled discretion from time to time to invest and reinvest the trust property in securities or any other kind of personal property, including, without limitation, shares of one or more of the Sentinel Funds, and to retain such investments and the original principal and any additions thereto indefinitely, even though any or all of the property retained is of a character or size which but for this express authority would not be considered a proper investment for a trustee.
(1) The most recent appointment made aforesaid shall bind the Trustee even if the Donor is not currently competent to exercise such right to appoint or remove. Each investment adviser shall accept appointment in a writing delivered to the Trustee. Each appointed adviser may resign at any time upon not less than thirty (30) days written notice to the Donor and the Trustee.
(2) While the Donor is living, the Donor shall be the investment adviser of any property for which another investment adviser has not been appointed. Each investment adviser, including the Donor, shall be a fiduciary hereunder as set forth in Section 3313 of the Delaware Code.
C. While an investment adviser is serving, the Trustee shall have no

responsibility whatsoever to consider the advisability of purchasing, retaining or disposing of any investment being managed by said adviser, except to determine that such investment could produce a reasonable return. If the Trustee determines that such an investment could not produce a reasonable return, the Trustee shall promptly notify the investment adviser of such determination, and the adviser shall have ten (10) days after such notice to sell said investment and reinvest the proceeds in accordance with Paragraph B above.

D. The Trustee shall have the power and authority to invest and reinvest the trust property set forth in Paragraph B above under any of the following circumstances:

(1) While the Donor is serving as investment adviser, after the Trustee has received written notice from the Donor's attending physician that the Donor is unable to manage his or her affairs,.with respect to the property being managed by the Donor.

(2) If a change of investment directed by the Trustee in accordance with the last sentence of Paragraph C does not occur as therein specified, with respect to such investment.

(3) After the death of the Donor.

(4) After its appointment as investment adviser pursuant to Paragraph B.

E. The Trustee shall pay from the trust property the compensation of each investment adviser other than the Donor.

ARTICLE V - TRUSTEE'S POWERS

Subject to Article IV above, the Trustee shall have the power and authority in its uncontrolled discretion, in addition to its powers conferred upon it by law and its other powers under this instrument:

A. To sell at public or private sale, exchange for like or unlike property, lease and otherwise dispose of and convey any property of the trust and to execute transfers, assignments, deeds, leases and other instruments of any kind.

B. To execute securities transactions without providing written confirmation thereof to the Donor or any beneficiary and to execute securities transactions through any broker or dealer, including an affiliate of the Trustee.

C. To vote directly and give discretionary or other proxies for voting any securities held hereunder, including shares of any investment company of which an affiliate of the trustee is investment adviser.

D. To join with other security holders in acting through committees, depositories, trustees or otherwise; to participate in any plan or proceeding, including any voting trust plan, for liquidating, protecting, or enforcing any right, obligation or interest arising from any property of the trust, or for reorganizing, consolidating, merging or adjusting the finances of any corporation, to accept in lieu thereof any new or substituted securities, whether of the same or a different kind or class, or with different priorities, rights or privileges, to pay any assessment or expense incident thereto, and to do any other act or thing that the Trustee may deem necessary or advisable in connection therewith. E. To make any division or distribution of trust property wholly or partly in cash or in kind, and to make reasonable and equitable valuations and apportionments thereof in connection with such a division or distribution.

F. To hold any or all trust property in its own name, as Trustee, in the name of a nominee or nominees or otherwise without indication of any trust, but in the event the same are held in its own name or in the name of a nominee or nominees, suitable indication is to be made upon the books and records of the Trustee that such property so held is part of the trust property; to keep trust property with a depository or custodian; and to keep trust property in book entry form.

G. To litigate, submit to arbitration, compromise or settle any claim in favor of or against the trust or any matter in controversy, and to execute all agreements, deeds and releases in connection therewith.

H. To employ, retain or consult accountants, investment counsel (and give them investment discretion), attorneys-at-law, other advisors and agents, and to pay compensation therefor and expenses in connection therewith from the trust without reduction of compensation otherwise payable to the Trustee except for investment counsel which is an affiliate of the Trustee.

I. Except as otherwise provided, to determine whether amounts received by the trust shall be allocated to principal or income, and to determine whether expenses, charges and liabilities incurred by the trust shall be charged against principal or income.

J. To commingle for convenience of administration any property of separate trusts hereunder with one another and with property of other trusts of which it is a trustee.

K. To reserve such reasonable amounts for any expenses, charges and liabilities, whether then accrued or estimated.

ARTICLE VI - GENERAL PROVISIONS

A. The interest of any beneficiary in either the income or principal of the trust shall not be alienated, anticipated or in any other manner assigned or transferred by such beneficiary; and such interest shall be free from interference or control by and exempt from execution, attachment, distress for rent and other legal or equitable process which may be instituted by or on behalf of any creditor, assignee or spouse of such beneficiary.

B. Whenever a beneficiary is entitled to a payment from the trust and the beneficiary is a minor, is ill, is incapacitated or is away, or because of other circumstances it is impractical or undesirable, in the Trustee's opinion, to make such payment directly to the beneficiary, the Trustee shall apply such payment for the beneficiary's benefit in such manner as the Trustee thinks best for the beneficiary. Such application for the beneficiary's benefit may be made directly or through such beneficiary's legal representative or a member of the beneficiary's family.

C. The receipt by a payee with respect to each payment of principal or income of the trust to such payee made in any manner specified in this instrument shall be a full discharge of the Trustee who shall not in any event be responsible for the subsequent application of any such payment.

D. The Trustee shall be entitled to reasonable compensation for its services hereunder, but not less than at the rates for trusts of a similar size and character contained in its schedule of fees it then publishes or quotes. In the event that the Trustee shall render any extraordinary services, it shall be entitled to additional compensation therefor. The Trustee shall be entitled to receive a fee in an amount equal to one percent of the fair market value of each distribution of the trust principal to beneficiaries other than the Donor.

E. Any Trustee may resign by delivery of a written resignation to the Donor and, after the Donor's death, to any beneficiary. The Donor may remove any Trustee by written notice specifying the date of removal. If a Trustee fails or ceases to act as Trustee, the Donor may by a writing appoint a successor Trustee. If the Donor fails to appoint a successor Trustee within thirty (30) days after the Trustee has resigned, a successor Trustee may be appointed by the Trustee so resigning upon written notice to any beneficiary. In the case of any vacancy in the office of Trustee hereunder not filled within sixty (60) days after such vacancy occurs, a successor Trustee may be appointed by any court having jurisdiction. No Trustee shall be liable for the actions, omissions or defaults of any prior Trustee nor have any responsibility to examine into the actions or omissions of any prior Trustee. Each successor Trustee shall be responsible only for property delivered to it by its predecessor Trustee. Each such appointment not made by a court shall take effect upon written acceptance of the office."

F. No one dealing with the Trustee shall be obliged to see to the application of money paid or property delivered to the Trustee or upon its order or to inquire into the necessity or propriety of Trustee exercising any of the powers conferred herein upon it, or to determine the existence of any fact upon which Trustee's power to perform any act hereunder may be conditioned. The Trustee shall not be required to give any bond or surety. The Trustee shall not be liable for errors of judgment or mistakes of fact or law, but only for willful defaults or gross negligence.

G. In the event the Trustee is unable or it is inconvenient for the Trustee to act with respect to any trust property, the Trustee shall have the power from time to time to designate in writing an individual or entity having trust powers, to act as Designated Trustee with respect such property. Each Designated Trustee shall have all of the Trustee's powers with respect to the specified property provided under this Agreement except as otherwise specified, and subject to any directions given from time to time in writing by the Trustee. Any Designated Trustee may resign at any time by delivery of a written resignation to the Trustee, and the Trustee may at any time by written notice remove the Designated Trustee.

H. Except as is necessary to determine if the investment is producing a reasonable return, the Trustee shall be under no duty to scrutinize the transactions or conduct of a Fund the shares of which are held hereunder, but shall cause a copy of each annual or other report when received from the Fund to be mailed to each beneficiary who is then entitled to a distribution from the trust. Such beneficiary (or if such beneficiary is not of full age and legal capacity, the beneficiary's legal representative or, if none, a parent of the beneficiary), and not the Trustee, shall have the right to assent or object to any transaction stated in such report or shown thereby and to bring any action against the Fund or the Fund's investment adviser that the Trustee might have brought on account of such a transaction.

I. The Trustee may from time to time render an account of its administration of the Trust hereunder to each beneficiary who during the period covered by the account was entitled absolutely to a distribution from the trust. Such account may be in the form of one or more statements of transactions. The written assent thereto of each such beneficiary shall fully protect the Trustee as to all matters or transactions stated in such account or shown thereby. Any beneficiary who is not of full age and legal capacity shall be deemed to assent to such account if his or her legal representative assents in writing to the account or if (the beneficiary having no such legal representative) any parent of the beneficiary assents in writing to the account. Any beneficiary to whom such account is rendered shall be deemed to assent to it unless he or she (or, if the beneficiary is not of full age and legal capacity, his or her legal representative or, if none, his or her parent) gives the Trustee written objection thereto within sixty (60) days after the account is rendered.

J. The taxable year of the trust shall be the calendar year.

K. This Agreement is made in, and shall be governed by, administered and interpreted in accordance with, the laws of the State of Delaware. However, the trustee is prohibited from exercising any power or discretion granted under said laws that would be inconsistent with the qualification of the trust under Section 664(d)(1) of the Code and the regulations promulgated thereunder.

ARTICLE VII - AFFILIATES

The Donor understands and agrees that National Life Insurance Company ("National Life") is indirectly the principal owner of AG&T and National Life or its affiliates may pay AG&T compensation related to the value of the trust's holdings of shares of the Funds; the investment adviser, transfer agent, principal underwriter and administrator of the Funds are affiliates of AG&T, and the Funds pay such affiliates compensation for their services to the Funds; and AG&T's compensation as Trustee will not be reduced by reason of any payment described above.

SIGNED this __________ day of ______________________, 2003.

WITNESS

____

___________________________(SEAL)

JOHN DOE, DONOR

The terms of this Agreement set forth the intentions of the donor and are in proper legal form.

____

Attorney for Donor (Signature)

____

Attorney's Name - Please Print

____

Street Address

____

City, State & Zip Code

AMERICAN GUARANTY & TRUST COMPANY, TRUSTEE

By:_____________________________________

JOHN DOE CHARITABLE REMAINDER ANNUITY TRUST

SCHEDULE A

____

$

STATE OF)
: SS.

COUNTY OF)
On this, the ______ day of ______________________, 2003, before me, the undersigned, a Notary Public in and for the State and County aforesaid, personally
appeared JOHN DOE, known to me to be the person whose name is subscribed to the
within instrument, and acknowledged that he executed the same for the purposes therein
contained.

IN WITNESS WHEREOF, I have hereunto set my hand and official seal.

____
NOTARY PUBLIC
STATE OF DELAWARE)
: SS.
COUNTY OF NEW CASTLE)
On this, the ______ day of ______________________, 2003 before me the undersigned, a Notary Public in and for the State and County aforesaid personally
appeared ____________________________, who acknowledged her/himself to be
____________________________ of AMERICAN GUARANTY & TRUST COMPANY, and
that s/he as such officer, being authorized to do so, executed the foregoing instrument for
the purposes therein contained by signing the name of AMERICAN GUARANTY &
TRUST COMPANY by her/himself as such.
IN WITNESS WHEREOF, I have hereunto set my hand and official seal.

____
NOTARY PUBLIC

SAMPLE LETTER OF WISHES

1 Physician Street
Your Town
U.S.A.

The Trustees
Your trust
Their Address

Today's date

Dear Sirs,

Your trust name

Updated Letter of Wishes

This is to state my wishes as to how I would like the above trust to be administered. These wishes are to be effective as from today and will supersede any issued before.

I wish this trust to be operated for the benefit of myself, **[Your name]**. In the event of bankruptcy or incapacity(whether physical, mental or legally/illegally imposed), I would like the trustees to operate in my perceived best interests. In the event of my death I would like you to operate the trust in the best interests of my wife and any children. If I am not married at the time of my death I would like the trust to operate for the benefit of **[your chosen heir, their address]**.

With regard to any property owned by the trust I would like it to be managed and rented with the trust to take the income unless the property it is required for the use of a beneficiary.

Yours sincerely

[Your name]

Summary

- A trust is an excellent method of preserving wealth across generations.
- A trust is a well respected and established wealth protection method.
- There are numerous different types of trust and you should consult and advisor as to which one is best for you.

8. Other methods

The more complicated it is to prove "clear" title to an asset the more difficult it is to seize. The following are some ways to achieve this.

DISCLAIMER

If you use any of these methods with the intent of defrauding another person(or entity), or depriving them of their rights or due assets then this is fraudulent and you may be punished accordingly. Using any of these methods to attempt to defeat a law suit currently in process, or that you believe will be filed may also invalidate the transfer and can be construed to be fraud.

However, if you have good title to an asset, have no fraudulent intent and are not expecting a claim against the asset then you are, of course, free to do whatever you like with it.

To show that there has been no fraud, you must show an intervening event, e.g. a law suit, accident or other *force majeure*(large and unexpected event).

Multiple titles

You do not have to hold the name of an asset in just one person or entity, you can have several. Having to go through the process of seizing the asset with several different entities(possibly in many different jurisdictions) can make the process, impossible, extremely difficult, or not worth justifying the cost of.

Clouded titles

Let's assume that somehow it may be possible for someone suing you to gain hold of an asset. You can make it infinitely less valuable to them by clouding the title. This makes it very difficult to sell on and much less valuable, so that it may not be worth going after. Clouding the title means making it unclear who actually owns, or controls the asset.

A good friend of mine is a fairly prosperous land owner, a while ago he thought he might get sued and took appropriate steps to protect his assets. He kept his land but took out a huge mortgage on it. Then he sold the farming rights to his wife and shooting rights to his son. Anyone managing to gain control of the property would find it to be nearly worthless as it can't be used for anything without all the attached rights. What rights can you sell to your property?

Liens

One of the first things my lawyer taught me was "don't kick an empty bucket", i.e. if someone doesn't have the money then it isn't worth suing them. If a guy has a $1M home with a $500K first mortgage and a $1M lien on it then what use is it to you to put your lien on after? There's no equity and the filing fees aren't worth the bother.

If you place a "friendly" lien on your assets then a creditor will have to wait in line before they stand a chance of seeing any money. If you register these liens then they will show on the report a Private Investigator will run prior to suing you. An attorney will see you owe far more then you own, are essentially bankrupt and it's not worth suing you. Also if you did go bankrupt he would have a long wait in line to get a penny.

Quit claims

These work similar to liens in which you quit your claim to an asset in favor of another party. You can choose whether you want to register them or not, but make sure they are properly notarized. I have one of these on my house, even though it's "in my name" I don't own it and it provides extra protection to the homestead protection already provided in Florida.

I did this so that I could still qualify easily for a mortgage, yet I still managed to transfer the asset into a corporation even though I didn't register the move or pay any sales taxes and fees. I managed this because I didn't sell it, I simply quit my claim to it.

Swiss Annuities

One of the soundest instruments for international asset protection are insurance products from Switzerland. This is because of powerful provisions in the Swiss insurance law.

In Swiss law, annuity and life insurance policies are fully protected and cannot be included in any bankruptcy procedure or seized by any creditors. Even if a foreign court should specifically order the seizure of a Swiss annuity account or its inclusion in a bankruptcy estate, the insurance policy will not be seized by the Swiss authorities, provided that it has been structured the right way.

Florida annunites are also protected from seizure from your creditors. However, you can't beat the extra level of comfort that 3,000 miles brings.

Action points

- Take all your equity out of each asset.
- Title all your assets so as to be worthless to anyone else.
- Documents can be notarized or prepared by a paralegal cheaply and will carry more apparent "weight"

Resources

- Lien document – to place a lien, or encumbrance on your asset.
- www.PracticeWithoutFear.com

Further reading

Summary

- Confusing a title and removing equity from an asset are quick and cheap ways to make assets less valuable or seizable to a creditor.

SAMPLE **ASSIGNMENT OF LIEN**

This assignment is made on [date] by [name of lienholder] , of [address] , City of [city] , County of [county] , State of [state] , herein referred to as "Assignor", to [name of assignee] , of [address] , City of [city] , County of [county] , State of [state], herein referred to as "Assignee". In consideration of [amount] Dollars, ($), receipt of which is hereby acknowledged, assignor does hereby assign to assignee the mechanic's lien on the property of [name of property owner] , located at [address] , [city] , [state] , which has been duly recorded in the office of [office], in Volume [number] , page , a copy of which is attached hereto.

9. Going offshore

Why go offshore?
In the event that the American justice system does fail, an offshore entity provides an extra level of comfort. If a judge can find an asset anywhere in their jurisdiction, i.e. the county, state, or country they can and will seize it, irrespective of the legality of that action. Isn't that illegal? Damn right it is, but what can you do about it if you can't appeal, don't have the money to appeal, or are held over a barrel in general. Even if you win and have the decision overturned it will take countless hours, crippling attorney fees and years off your life.

What is offshore?
Offshore simply means a different country, or jurisdiction. To a European the US is an "offshore" jurisdiction. In fact in some instances for foreign investors the US is an excellent tax haven. The Federal government gives significant tax breaks and incentives to encourage foreign investment here.

Going offshore is the big boy of all asset protection strategies. No matter what a domestic court may order in a civil matter a good offshore jurisdiction simply couldn't care less and will happily ignore any communication from them. Going offshore may bring all kinds of additional benefits including, but not limited to:

- Nominee directors
- Bearer shares(the holder of the share is the owner)
- No share register
- No need to file annual accounts
- No tax

- No records of directors

The combination of one, or more of the above can make it extremely difficult to find you have anything to do with the corporation, let alone try to seize it, or any of its assets.

If you place assets offshore they cannot be in your name. A Federal judge can and will demand that you repatriate your assets and mail jail you if you do not do so. If assets are not in your name a "request" for their repatriation is usually sufficient to satisfy a court.

The costs of setting up an offshore company are usually quite low(very low 4 figures) and on going maintenance should run you just over $1,000 per year. Taking your P.A. offshore would have significant asset protection benefits, but would probably draw unwelcome attention from the IRS. You may wish to use a corporation like this for consulting work, to hold liens over your assets, license intellectual property or provide financing(at high interest rates).

Tax

There may be some tax benefits to be realized by shifting your income and/or assets offshore, some of which may be considerable. However, you should consult with a qualified professional before making any tax decision as the IRS are some of the last people on earth you want to be on the wrong side of.

Terrorism and public perception of offshore entities

The public at large has a poor perception of offshore jurisdictions, this is mainly unfounded and encouraged by revenue collecting governments as a new "bogey man" to be afraid of. There is nothing, in itself, illegal about an offshore entity. Some may be used for illegal purposes, as an on shore entity could also be, but like the NRA says "Guns don't kill people. People kill people."

Public perception can occasionally be harmful, or a nuisance to you. Following the events of September 11th there has been a major crackdown on offshore entities. This poor perception may make it difficult to do business with other corporations, or to secure financing. You may also find tightening regulations make using the entity more difficult, or require more disclosure than you are comfortable with.

Jurisdictions:
The tax, legal, cost and operational aspects of an offshore corporation or trust can be complex and often change. You should consult with your offshore company formation agent prior to making your choice. Have in mind a good idea of what you would like to use the entity for and run it by the agent to make sure the jurisdiction and type of entity are suitable for your needs.

You should continually monitor the countries you decide to use as an asset base as changing laws and treaties may produce a climate that becomes unsuitable for your needs, necessitating a change of jurisdiction. The Sovereign Society produces an excellent monthly magazine to help keep you abreast of changes in the offshore world(don't have it sent to your home or office). The following is a rough overview of different jurisdictions to help you narrow down your choices before doing further research.

There are many other countries that may qualify as an offshore asset repository that are not included below. These are countries like Malta, Luxembourg, Singapore, Gibraltar, Hong Kong, Dubai, etc. We have not included them here as they are not generally considered to be good "all round" jurisdictions for asset protection and international business purposes.

Jurisdiction	**Comments**
Liberia and other African countries	Liberia has an excellent legal framework for registering companies, ships and aircraft that is based on the same laws as Panama. It is excellent for privacy and ease of use. However this, and any other African jurisdiction reek of fraud and should be avoided. Political instability is also a major factor
Switzerland and Lichtenstein	Despite what you may have heard Switzerland is no longer the safe, private, asset repository it once was. New laws and treaties have made the old Switzerland a thing of the past. The "new" Switzerland is

	Lichtenstein. It's expensive, but is one of the best and most professional asset bases available.
Nauru and The Cook Islands	These are South Pacific based jurisdictions, home to many "banks" and are a little too esoteric and exotic for physicians.
The Isle of Man and Channel Islands	These are British dependencies with excellent communication and legal infrastructure. Pressure from the European Union is eroding their sovereignty and usefulness, so I would think twice before using them as a base.
The Bahamas	Close to the US, fairly secure
Panama	Excellent corporate and trust law, a very good choice
Belize	Cheap and quick to set up corporations and trusts. Slightly tarnished reputation, but very flexible.
Aruba, Bermuda and Barbados	Reporting restrictions and lack of bank secrecy make these poor offshore choices
The British Virgin Islands	Too close to the US government for US citizens to consider.
Cayman Islands	Used to be a very discrete, safe, choice. However, recent treaties with the US government have made it a poor choice for anyone desiring secrecy.
Nevis & St. Kitts and Turks & Caicos	Bank secrecy, a decent asset haven, but they both run a little on "island time".
Austria	Not really a tax haven, but a great banking jurisdiction.

Captive offshore insurance companies

Low risk and fed up of high premiums? Then why not self insure? A highly successful physician, or a group of physicians can get together and form an offshore captive insurance company, which can then in turn, insure them. The insurance company needs a large amount of capital to start, this is secured by you and/or your colleagues and the company will then take a lien, or ownership over the assets to provide this. This is a good first layer of asset protection.

Your insurance payments are tax deductible and any money residing offshore, not repatriated to the U.S. and not owned by you is also usually tax free(consult an experienced CPA regarding this). Money paid to the insurance company is money that you no longer have to lose in a law suit(layer number two).

Finally a lawyer will realize that an offshore company may be considerably less likely to pay up, and will be very difficult to pressure to do so. This may well make them think twice before filing a suit(layer three).

Resources:
www.PracticeWithoutFear.com

Company and trust formation:
www.apfpconsulting.com
www.ocra.com
www.scfgroup.com
www.icsl.com
www.offcorp.com
www.globalmoney.com

Offshore banks:
www.axxess-international.com
www.bancop.dk
www.cortal.fr
www.ebanking.com
www.bgl.lu

www.anoffshore.com
www.volksbankdirekt.at
www.united-bank.net

Don't forget that you should declare any offshore bank account containing over $10,000 on your tax return. Of course, if you don't own it then you don't have to. You may also not want to have mail from "Bank of hidden assets" delivered to your house, so we suggest you open a mail box in another town, preferably with a private company(and obviously be sure to use the correct ID!). Many offshore banks will also hold your mail for you.

Further reading

- The bumper book of bank applications – Patrick Torrent
- Banking in silence – W.G. Hill
- The tax haven report – Adam Starchild

Summary

- An offshore corporation is very difficult for creditors to pursue
- An offshore company has significant privacy and asset protection benefits

10.Ultimate privacy

Of course the ultimate method of asset protection is for no one to know about them and them not to be in your name. Why won't a lawyer or accountant tell you this? Simple, there's no money in it for them. They can't sell you an expensive trust, or charge you large on going fees for maintaining a complicated corporate structure.

Isn't this totally illegal?
John Wayne, Elton John, Sting and Tom Cruise are just some of the people that don't use the names they were born with, you can too. Writers use pen names all the time to protect their identify. Is Madonna a criminal for using an assumed name? No, and neither are you if your intent is not to defraud or deceive.

Identification:
Of course, just calling yourself by a different name is not necessecarily enough in today's world, you'll need some ID. Fortunately help is at hand, there are plenty of alternative ID producers, just ask your teenage kid... We've included a list of them in the resources section.

Once you've got yourself some new ID you can have a open bank accounts(you may like to set up a mail drop first) and buy things.

Portable Wealth:
Talking of buying things you can easily purchase some very expensive and small items that don't have to be registered, hold their value well, or appreciate and can easily be sold. Some items you might like to consider are:

- Gold(silver is too bulky for the price). Purchased of gold in the USA must be registered(presumably for tax reasons and in case the government decides to confiscate it, as they have done before.) Make sure to give the "proper" information and ID when making your purchases.
- Platinum
- Colored diamonds(the market for clear ones is no longer supported and prices are dropping here).
- Antiques

- Watches - Big names like Rolex and the complications(fine hand made watches with extensive, complicated movements) from established Swiss manufacturers are good here.
- Bearer bonds and stock certificates
- Traveler's cheques
- Airline tickets(yes, that's right. They're as good as cash, can be traded in at any time, one ticket can easily be worth a small fortune with several long haul first class connections and it attracts no attention at an airport)

Banks, brokerages, car, boat and plane dealers, etc are all required to report cash transactions over $10,000. Of course not all of them do, but that's another story. If you spread the amounts over smaller transactions to avoid this limit, you can be charged with "structuring", so be careful not to do this either.

Looks like a bank, acts like a bank...
There are places where you can open an account with no ID, no social security number, in any name whatsoever and sometimes with no address needed. They're called utility companies, mobile phone providers, secured credit cards, etc. As long as you're not planning on defrauding them you can do whatever you want. Simply "pre-pay" your bill and you have a "deposit". They can make payments for you by your phoning up and asking them to send you a check for some of your positive balance in pretty much any name you want.

Numbered accounts
Several banks offshore offer numbered accounts where your name is not even required to open them. If they can't be proven to belong to you they can't be seized can they? Countries with an adversarial relationship to the U.S, like China are unlikely to divulge your details under pressure. Never use a Swiss bank, they leak information like sieves and will roll over on you to the IRS for "finders" fees. The Swiss banking myth is just that. If you want old world secure banking try Lichtenstein or Austria instead.

Shut up:
Don't say a word. Loose lips sink ships. Keep Schtum. Keep quiet. Don't tell us, don't tell your lawyer, don't tell your spouse, don't tell your kids, don't tell your dog.

> The only way for two people to keep a secret is if one of them is dead.
> – Benjamin Franklin

If no one knows where you've put your cash they can't find it. If they can find it they can't take it.

Action points

- Do your due diligence
- Put some money away for a rainy day

Resources:
www.PracticeWithoutFear.com
www.investmentrarities.com
www.2020tech.com/maildrop/privacy.htm
www.ptshamrock.com
www.freebooter.com
www.2nd-passports.com

Further reading

- Hide your assets and disappear – Edmund J. Pankau
- Fugitive – Ken Abaygo
- Advanced Fugitive – Ken Abaygo
- International Fugitive – Ken Abaygo
- The Paper Trip I – Eden Press
- The Paper Trip II – Eden Press
- The Paper Trip III – Eden Press
- Bullet Proof Asset Protection – William S. Reed J.D.
- International identity change – Newborn
- Who are you – Scott French
- The bumper book of bank applications – Patrick Torrent
- Privacy and how to get it – Eden Press
- How to Disappear in America – Eden Press

- How to disappear completely and never be found – Doug Richmond

Summary

- The simple solution may often be the best
- You should do your due diligence before committing your assets
- Plan ahead
- Keep quiet

11. Getting sued – your response

First, relax and take a deep breath. If you lose control of yourself you lose control of the situation. Sit down and take stock of the situation. Remember how we told you about fitting into the category where you're not worth suing? When they see that a contingency lawyer is going to go and look for lower hanging fruit. They may write you a few nasty letters, but basically if they can't get anything(which they can't if you've done your job right with protecting your assets) then they'll go away.

Get yourself an attorney. Ask around and hire someone noted for their tenacity and mindless aggression. You should always try to pay your attorney a flat fee with a strong success related element rather than an hourly rate as this drastically reduces their incentive to "run their clock" on you. Either have him write to the other side explaining your side of things(they don't really care about this) and explaining that you have no assets and are deeply in debt(they do care about that). Your mantra throughout is "I DON'T HAVE ANY ASSETS." You own nothing, remember?

You may like to consider printing up a leaflet like the following, which I have entitled "So you're thinking of filing a frivolous lawsuit". I had a bunch of these printed off at Kinkos and have them in a dispenser on my desk and a few in my car. The attorneys I have shown them to think they're very funny and that I'm a lunatic.

Only two types of people would have something like this: Someone who gets sued all the time and knows all the tricks or a madman. No one in their right mind wants to sue any one of them. You may like to make up your own version and get it professionally printed, if only for your personal amusement.

Without prejudice
Private & Confidential
Not for publication

So, you're thinking of filing a frivolous lawsuit?

Against

Doctor X

or an associated entity

The abundance of nuisance law suits is of great concern, whilst deciding whether to file or continue yours you might like to bear the following points in mind:

- Doctor X has no assets.
- Doctor X has no income.
- Doctor X vigorously defends his legal rights.
- Doctor X's lawyers are amongst the World's foremost experts on asset protection.
- Persons involved with action against Doctor X, or an associated entity, who exceed their mandate are often prosecuted personally.
- His consultancy work for extra national organizations gives him sovereign immunity from prosecution in any jurisdiction under the Vienna convention.
- He comes from one of America's most distinguished business families who can trace their roots back to the 17th Century. His reputation is beyond reproach.

- **Doctor X has never lost a lawsuit.**

In order to assist you in planning any legal action a handy check list has been included below:

- Find someone or something to sue(not always as easy as it first appears).
- See if there are any assets not attached or with any equity(most lawyers know not to "kick an empty bucket").
- Attempt to verify if title to the asset is clear(difficult and unlikely).
- File a lawsuit in the relevant country in the relevant language using local counsel(good luck with this, you will need it)
- Win the lawsuit (unlikely).
- Repeat the process again in whatever jurisdiction the assets have been transferred to.

About Doctor X

Doctor X is an acknowledged expert on asset protection and International business. He is often consulted by multi national corporations, high net worth individuals and performs consultancy work for extra national organizations.

Whilst he dislikes legal action he is extremely well prepared for the type of threats that unfortunately plague our society. Hence he has never lost a lawsuit.

If you believe you have a legitimate complaint you are advised to talk it out in a polite and constructive manner, if not please consider the proceeding.

Action points

- Keep calm
- Get an attorney
- Respond
- Always say you have no assets

Resources:

www.PracticeWithoutFear.com
So, you're thinking of filing a frivolous law suit leaflet
www.martindale.com

Further reading

www.nolo.com

Summary

- If you have no assets you can't lose them
- If you have no assets you're not really worth suing
- No law suit is ever fun

12. Other tricks

Not everyone plays fair and there's no reason why you should too. This is your livelihood at stake and all's fair in love and war. Screw them before they screw you, etc...

Interviewing
Once you've interviewed a lawyer about representing you in a matter he can't them take a case against you. Find who the "A list" players are in town and go and see them all, it will mean your opponent can't use them.

Diplomatic immunity
Don't laugh. Diplomatic immunity isn't just for the Latinos with Zero Halliburton cases and it's more common than you'd think. If you perform an action for an embassy or diplomat you enjoy limited immunity whilst you perform that action. I enjoy limited diplomatic protection through consulting work I do for a United Nations affiliate organization.

You can even become a Honary consul. Representation abroad is very expensive for countries and most will consider appointing a local of good reputation to act as a trade liaison, help issue visas and act as a point of contact for its nationals in need locally. If you are willing to do this you too can enjoy diplomatic immunity which extends to your house, office, cars, etc. A diplomat can't be sued unless you initiate the action in which case you waive your right to immunity for that matter.

Paying a claim
If you can show that you are unable to pay a claim, you may be able to negotiate it lower. A patient may well accept this lower offer as they will look to go after you at a later date for the rest. Pay the claim, plus a little bit extra, e.g. $10,027.36 for a $10,000 settlement and include a settlement letter. The extra money is consideration for their undertaking not to pursue you further. Most people will cash the check without reading the letter properly and will assume the extra money is a simple "rounding error".

This nicely kicks in the legal doctrine of "estoppel". This basically means that they can't pursue you, as they're not allowed to do something they've agreed not to do.

Filing bankruptcy
You can use this to escape from creditors, though not all your debts, especially government and court imposed sanctions may be wiped out. States like Texas and Florida have generous homestead allowances meaning you can keep your home in spite of bankruptcy(as long as you keep paying your property taxes). This is an involved and complicated process and not one you should undertake lightly, if at all. The threat of bankruptcy, if properly used, may well force a plaintiff to think twice.

Attaching wages
Different states have differing regulations regarding what earnings may be garnished and how. You may like to consider writing the contract and receiving the income in a state friendly to your needs.

Don't earn it personally.
The safest way of all is not to earn any income at all. Have it directed to a separate company, or trust. If you don't earn it, it can't be seized.

Competency
If you were not competent at the time you signed any document then it has no validity, or legal force. For example if you have signed a document whilst under the influence of prescribed psychogenic drugs, alcohol or sleep deprivation then you might like to look at re-evaluating what you have signed. As you know, medical documentation will be required for this.

If your incapacitation is permanent, or may last some time you can appoint, or have appointed someone to manage your affairs for you.

Legal ways to change or alter your name
Use a different name. How does Robert Jones relate to Ian Clarke or Peter Smith? You can being using a different name simply by adopting it as one of your aliases, you don't even have to file any legal documents. Actors do this all the time as a stage name. You can use your middle name, an ethnic spelling of your name or combinations of the above to confuse records. If you were adopted you may use your former name and many states will issue you a new birth certificate to match. Get as many documents in your new names as possible.

Disappear:
If things get too much you could always just up and leave. We don't necessarily advocate this, but you should consider it as an option. It's nice to know that you still have options left when your back is to the wall. If you do decide to do this then you should lay extensive plans to do so as the more time you spend planning the more successful your "new life" is likely to be.

If you disappear to another country make sure you have not committed any criminal acts. Most countries will only extradite you for criminal actions, not civil ones. If you are worried about being repatriated do not go to a country that has US troops stationed there as these jurisdictions have negotiated civil treaties with the countries. You may like to consider an unconventional border crossing at a small outpost that will not have scanners sending your passport information back to Washington, e.g. small airports and docks. Lastly never use a bank that has US branches, the government can and will pressure them to release your funds, or give up information about you.

Action points:

Resources:
www.PracticeWithoutFear.com

Further reading:
- Part time diplomacy – James Basil-Hart
- Above the law – Ambassador X
- Everything about diplomatic passports, diplomatic status, honorary consulates and related matters – Global money consultants
- Asset protection secrets – Arnold Goldstein

Summary:

- You should consider every option available to you to protect your assets.
- The more creative the solution the less experience an attorney will have countering it.

13. Summary and acting now

Asset protection is very simple.

Pay attention here:

<u>If you don't own it then you can't lose it.</u>

This is very important so let's go over it again:
If YOU don't own it then YOU can't lose it.

All the expensive advice you can buy and any book essentially boils down to this point. If you bear this in mind in every financial transaction you make you won't go far wrong.

All this sounds good, right? Well it is, as long as you actually do it. Just buying this book won't protect your assets. Only you can do that. Start now. Plan what you want to do, do your research, fill out your forms, call your legal advisors and company/trust formation agents.

Here is a handy comparison chart of option available to you:

Asset Protection comparison chart

Method	Cost	Effectiveness	Complexity	Risk
Donating your assets	You get a tax write off	Total – no longer yours	Simple	Low
Giving your assets away	Free	Depends who you give them to	Simple	Low to moderate
Quitclaim	Minimal	Depends who you quit claim to	Simple	Low to Moderate
Selling your assets	You make money	Depends who you sell them to	Simple	Low to moderate
Loan against accounts receivable	Interest on the loan	High, a lawyer has to get through the bank as the first lien	Moderate to high	Moderate
Blanket insurance policy	Variable	Variable	Variable	Variable
Pre-marital agreement	High	Moderate to low	Medium to high	Moderate
Give away your 401K	Free	Depends who you give it to	Medium to low	Moderate
Corporation	Moderate	Moderate to Good	Moderate to high	Moderate
Offshore corporation	Moderate to high	Good to excellent	Moderate to high	Low
Revocable trust	Moderate to high	Useless	Moderate to high	Just send them a cheque
Irrevocable trust	Moderate to high	Good to excellent	High	Low to very low
Charitable remainder trust	High	Good to moderate	High	Moderate
Offshore	Moderate to High	Laugh while they try to get	High	Lower than an

irrevocable trust		through this one		ambulance chaser's ethics
Life insurance annuity	High	Moderate	Moderate to low	Moderate
Swiss Annuity	High	High	Moderate	Low
Lien	Low	Depends who places the lien	Moderate	Moderate
Assignment of rights(clouding title)	Low	Depends on what you've done	The more complex, the better	Moderate
Offshore captive insurance company	High	Moderate to high	High	Moderate to low
Offshore bank account	Low	Depends on the ownership, the location and who knows about it	Low	Depends on the ownership, the location and who knows about it
Bank account – other name	Low	Excellent, if kept quiet	Moderate to high	Excellent, if kept quiet
Portable wealth	Whatever you want to spend	Good	Low	Good if kept quiet
Offshore numbered account	Low	Excellent, if kept quiet	Moderate	Excellent, if kept quiet
Keeping quiet(total secrecy)	Low	High	You boast, you're broke	You boast, you're broke, otherwise low
Diplomatic appointment	High	High	High	Low to moderate
Bankruptcy	High	Moderate to high	High	High

Disappear	High	Depends on your intelligence, your preparation and your commitment	High	High
Retire	High – no more income	Total – your working income is gone	Low	Low
Hire a lawyer	High	Low	High	Much higher than his fees

In short, DO SOMETHING and DO IT NOW. Next week never comes and may be too late for you. The sooner you do something the sooner you can sleep well at night.

Good luck.

14. Case Studies

The following case studies are actual accounts of physicians, the names and some details have been changed to protect their privacy. We will first explain to you:

1. The situation
2. The outcome
3. What the physician could have done to change the outcome.

Malpractice vs. Mal outcome

The situation

Physician AB has a 30 year old mother of three small girls present with a one day history of big, diffuse, non-specific, non-localizing, abdominal cramps. Review of systems and records were completely non-contributory, stool was negative for blood and a CBC and sed rate were within normal limits. Patient was aferile and sent home with abdominal muscle relaxants and advised to follow a clear liquid diet.

That night she presented herself to the ER with the same complaints, again the exam was non-specific, a repeat CBC was performed with no change and a upper GI was performed. She was sent home with instructions for a clear liquid diet and to see her FP in the AM. She presented to her FP in the AM with the same complaints and no change in her clinical exam. The upper GI was read as negative, another CBC, sed rate, amylase and lipase were drawn and patient was sent home.

Early the following morning her husband found her dead in bed. The subsequent lab work all proved to be normal and the upper GI was read as normal. The autopsy revealed the patient died of strep sepsis.

The Outcome

The family practitioner, the emergency room physician and the radiologist were each sued for $1M, the extent of their malpractice insurance. The insurance carriers decide to settle within one year for the full amount of each physician. The plaintiff's attorney recommended settlement.

Discussion

This is a case of mal outcome and not necessarily malpractice. As any physician can see, there was no clinical or laboratory indication, or reason this lady should have had strep sepsis, but she did, and she died. The family physician ordered all the appropriate testing and had complete negative clinical exams. The emergency room physician likewise performed the usual standard of care and the radiologist read the upper GI correctly.

The physicians' attorneys felt that the emotional impact of the patient's young children in tears on a witness stand would, more than likely, override any scientific logic in the eyes of a jury. All three physicians were subsequently dropped by their insurance carrier, are now paying exorbitant rates and, at the time of this law suit, none of them had adequate asset protection.

They have subsequently all put their affairs in order, having learned why they needed to the hard way. All three physicians were lucky that there was \$3M of insurance money, because under the laws of their state the attorney is entitled to 30% of the first million, 20% of the second and 10% of the third million, plus expenses. Therefore any settlement over \$3M is irrelevant in the attorney's eyes. As we can see the attorney made \$600,000 plus expenses for a few months work for a case of mal outcome, not malpractice.

Too honest for his own good

Situation

CD was a 45 year old physician, who was the father of two children in college and a solo physician with a thriving practice. Both he and his wife realize that their marriage has deteriorated to platonic tolerance. He, on the other hand, had fallen in platonic love with his nurse for the past five years. He wished to end his current marriage as soon as possible and begin his new life with his nurse.

Outcome

Wishing to finalize matters in a polite, fair and speedy manner, he therefore approached his wife with the situation. He offered her all of their accumulated assets during their marriage in consideration of a speedy divorce. They agree and he signs over all of his assets to her. She subsequently talks to an embittered, divorced physician's wife who advises her to see a very aggressive attorney for maximum alimony. She is subsequently awarded maximum alimony and gets to keep all of the assets because she agreed to a speedy divorce for consideration of all the assets. He falsely assumed that meant no alimony.

Discussion

- Always document every agreement in writing.
- Always ensure the other party is represented by adequate legal counsel in any negotiation.
- Ensure that any settlement contains a "no pursuing" clause.
- Never <u>assume</u> anything in a divorce.
- Don't have affairs at the office.
- Never assume you know your wife until the end of a divorce

Never take your eye off the ball...

The situation

Doctor EF, a 50 year old family physician was doing a routine stress test on a very healthy looking and actively exercising 55 year old executive. The patient and physician have had a long standing relationship for the past 15 years and the executive has never had any illnesses other than routine colds and flu's. In the recent past he and physician EF had played a vigorous game of tennis together.

During the stress test the physician and technician were both in the room through stage 2 Bruce protocol. The physician's nurse then came in the room and interrupted him to take a call from the mother of a child he had seen in the emergency room the night before. Knowing that he had played tennis with the patient less than a month ago and the patient's dedication to personal fitness, he felt secure in leaving the room to take the call.

Somewhere between five an ten minutes later he was summoned back into the room to evaluate his friend who was obviously undergoing an acute MI. All appropriate cardiac resuscitation measure were instituted but the patient died within five minutes.

The outcome

The patient's wife, the executor of his estate, sued the doctor, who was carrying $250K/$750K malpractice insurance. The insurance carrier settled their $250K and the case went to trial. The wife was awarded $6M in lost wages and punitive damages. The physician had to sell all of his assets and a large portion of his salary is attached for the remainder of his working career.

Discussion

- It is far easier to set up an asset protection plan before the event, as afterwards there may be nothing to protect.
- We recommend that your retirement accounts are not in your name.
- His home and all of his assets should not have been in his name.

- Had his income gone to another corporation it could not have been attached as easily.
- All of his stocks and bonds could have been in a non-attachable annuity.
- Had he bought a whole life insurance policy rather than term life, he would have had a growing asset that could not be attached.

The yellow devil…

GH is an extremely successful surgeon. He has all the trappings of wealth… including a bright yellow Lamborghini Diablo(oh, and he also had a teenage daughter). Now you all know what's going to happen next, so fast forward to her and a friend trying to outrun a train across a rail road crossing at approx. 120 mph.

They all wake up in hospital with external injuries and the girl's parents file suit.

The outcome

Fortunately he has a $2M umbrella insurance policy and the girl's parents just so happen to sue him for $2M. The insurance company pays and most of them live happily ever after.

Discussion

- An umbrella insurance policy is a wise thing to have.
- If you have a teenager this applies doubly to you. Both of the authors have gone joyriding in their parent Ferraris and Mercedes having surreptitiously removed them from their garages.
- Please make sure that your cars are not registered in your name.
- Whether you give permission to your child to take the car or not, you are still liable for any incident.
- When we were taught to drive we were told that one of our friends learning in the same year would die in an automobile accident. Try not to let this be your child.

Scorned but rich...

Situation

IJ, a 55 year old solo surgeon physician with an extremely lucrative practice, 3 children in college, 2 in high school has a 24 year marriage that has been deteriorating for 10 years. The wife has been primarily a stay at home mother and has built her self image on the success of her husband. IJ naively thinks that this can be a 50/50 split of assets and that the two can remain friends for their children. After they separate the wife interviews with 12 divorce lawyers and hires the most aggressive attorney in town who, naturally, exacerbates the situation.

Forged signatures appear on quit claim deeds, IJ is accused of stealing from his practice and even molesting his daughter. IJ is amazed at the different woman he is now dealing with.

Outcome

IJ loses all of his assets, including his office, retirement account and half of his practice. She receives maximum alimony for life and ends up with substantially larger monthly passive income than his working income.

Discussion

- Make copies of all documents including deeds, taxes(for 5 years) before a divorce.
- Put your office building, practice and as many assets as you can in a trust for your children, or designated heir.
- Remove all documents to a safe place.
- Divorce settlements are rarely equitable. Judges typically rule disproportionately in favor of one party. Trial have little to do with justice, but "truth management". Heinous allegations are merely lawyer tactics to keep you off guard and unfocussed.

No good deed goes unpunished…

Situation

KL is a nephrologist. He was finishing his afternoon rounds, walking down the hallway on the way to the garage when he heard a young nurse screaming for help. He found her giving mouth to mouth resuscitation and immediately starts cardiac compression. By this time other nurses have called a code, a crash cart appears, appropriate drugs are given and the patient survives. The patient is then taken to ICU where she continues to live for two months. He later finds out that she was a DNR.

Outcome

There is a large family dispute over the DNR status and some members of the family are extremely distraught with their mother's condition. The hospital bills exceed $500K, the family sues for lost wages, pain and suffering, etc. Dr KL is sued for $3M and taken to court, an award of $1M is awarded against him and his malpractice insurance of $250K settles. He sells all his assets and takes a loan out for the remainder. He will spend the next five years paying off his loan.

Discussion

- If you have assets, you are a target.
- Put assets protection plans in place BEFORE you need them.
- Good Samaritan laws are now, for the most part, null and void as attorneys have repeatedly gone right through them.
- Doing the right thing is sometimes the wrong thing.
- Each physician should consult with their medical staff to check if they are covered and what the hospital policy on such an issue is.

Killed by his own kindness…

Situation

MN was an OB/GYN who had been in the same practice with the same nurse for 25 years. Over this time they had become close, would often work until 7 or 8 at night(with no overtime paid to the nurse). He would discuss his marital issues with her and would often hug her, or place an arm around her during the course of the day. He would frequently walk in public with his arm around her shoulder. The relationship remained asexual and she never married during this time. Unfortunately, she had strong feelings for him and assumed that when he retired he would leave his wife for her. They never discussed this. When he finally retired and did not leave his wife she visited a lawyer and brought suit against him for sexual harassment and back dated overtime with interest(at the lawyer's suggestion).

Outcome

He went to trial and was cleared of sexual harassment, however it ruined his reputation and ended his marriage. He was assessed for back overtime with interest for a total of $2.3M, which was the majority of his retirement account. The remained of his assets were unequally divided in the divorce and he ended up essentially destitute in retirement.

Discussion

- ALWAYS retain a professional relationship with all female staff members.
- Things that happen during your career can come back to bite you afterwards.
- NEVER discuss personal matters with professional staff.
- Keep meticulous records of any overtime, or any time that members of your family, or friends, put in to a practice.
- His retirement fund should not have been in his name.
- The remainder of his assets should have been placed in trust.

Stick to what you know

Situation

OP is a 36 year old family physician, who has a fast growing practice. He is introduced by one of his patients to the "new big thing", a home water ozoneator. He becomes very excited about the product and it's potential good for both his patients and to him financially. He started recommending it, then selling it in his office. He is asked to join the board of the ozoneator company and enthusiastically agrees. Several years go by, during which time he continues to recommend both the product and the company's stock. He makes a lot of money on all fronts.

A government study is released which claims that the product has virtually no validity. Many of his patients start to demand their money back from him and he gets sued by some for recommending the stock.

Outcome

The court finds him liable for mixing his medical practice with the promotion of the company and its product, especially since he is a director. Those people who were both investors and patients sue him corporately and the court upholds their claim because they brought a medical product through his office and he recommended it to them as their physician.

Discussion

- He should have obtained adequate director's liability insurance.
- He could have held the directorship in a corporate name.
- He should not have promoted, or sold, the product in his office.
- Any recommendation of the product, or the company's stock should have been clearly marked as his position as a board director.
- Make clear that any recommendations you make are not as a physician.
- Do not mix any involvement in a MLM promotion with your practice of medicine.

Hoist by his own petard…

Situation

QR is a family physician with an excellent reputation and a very busy practice, who had never been sued. One day he saw a patient who presents with symptoms of a URI. The examination shows pustular exudates in the throat and strep test confirms streptococcus. The patient is treated appropriately with penicillin, but 24 hours later presents to the emergency room in an obtunded state. The patient is found to have streptococcul meningitis. The patient survives, but is left permanently deaf.

QR is sued, and when he reviews his records found that he had not noted the patient's neck was supple even though he had performed this test and found it to be fine. Since he only uses the same type of cheap, disposable, pen to write his notes he adds "neck supple" to the chart.

Outcome

A spectrophotometric ink test is performed on the chart and the words, "neck supple" are found to have been from a different batch of ink, with a color difference that is not visible to the naked eye and must, therefore, have been added later. It is assumed that QR did not perform this test and is sued for: 1.Altering medical records; 2.Not performing an adequate clinical test and 3.Missed diagnosis. This is an indefensible law suit and he loses – BIG.

Discussion

- If you learn nothing else from this book – NEVER ALTER MEDICAL RECORDS. If he had simply done nothing he would have had the benefit of reasonable doubt, his own actions cost him his career.
- Records can be tested for different ink. Your handwriting also differs constantly with factors like stress, the position you were writing it(seated or standing) and the surface you are writing on. Whilst this is not a 100% exact science, it can add doubt to an already shaky situation.
- He should have the WITHOUT PREDJUDICE disclaimer at the top of all his notes. He can then decide that can be used in court and what cannot.

- He should shred any old documents over 7 years old, you never know when an old case can bite you.

The test that cost more than you bargained for...

Situation

ST is an internist who had a young woman present to his office wanting a pre-marital HIV and STS drawn. She had been promiscuous for many years and now wished to settle down and marry. The STS came back first and the nurse called the patient to inform her that it was negative, marking "patient called re test results" in the patient's chart. The HIV test came in the following week and a different nurse noted it in the chart and observed that she had already been called re test results. Assuming that this was for both she took no action.

The patient subsequent got married and pregnant in the ensuing year and during routine blood work from her obstetrician was found to be HIV positive. Knowing that she had had an HIV test less than 12 months before, she enquired as to its results to confirm her belief that her husband had given it to her. She was shocked to find out the truth and later lost both husband and baby.

Outcome

She sued the physician. There being no defense he lost. Financially and professionally ruined he became more and more depressed, eventually committing suicide by shooting himself.

Discussion

- All employees should be independent contractors.
- All employees should carry their own insurance. Whilst he would still probably have been sued if the above points were carried out, the severity of the judgment would have been lessened.
- When you terminate an employee have them sign a separation release agreement

The World is not flat...

Situation

UV was a cancer specialist recruited by a major hospital chain to be an in house oncologist. During his cancer research he wrote a paper charting the cellular evolution of a particular cancer cell showing that it evolved over many millennia. The hospital chain was a religious organization that believed in "special creation". They asked him to retract his paper as it went against their view that the earth is only a few thousand year old and was created as a whole. He refused. Since the research was done under the name of the facility they threatened to sue him.

Outcome

He counter sued stating that scientific facts and established dogma superceded religious beliefs. The hospital not wanting to undergo another Scopes trial they settled by dropping their law suit and paying for his relocation.

Discussion

Certain people and institutions who you may deal with may have political and/or religious views that may be in conflict with your own, or with your practice of medicine. You should thoroughly evaluate any situation in advance that may pose a conflict with your belief systems, particularly is strongly held.

The physician that represents himself has a fool for a client.

Situation

WX has been a physician for 35 years and usually responded to his ER call in a belated fashion. On one occasion the back up physician was so angry at his repeated tardiness that he complained to the DPR.

WX feeling this was a nuisance issue, and being aware of another physician(whom he considered had done something much worse) getting a "slap on the wrist", decided to represent himself.

Outcome

WX had his license suspended for a period of time.

Discussion

The other physician was represented by an attorney, who understood the full legalities of his situation and was able to make a proper plea bargain. The board, not wishing to get into a legal dispute, was careful to follow it's guidelines.

WX had no idea of the guidelines, the rules and governance of arbitration, or legal proceedings in these matters. He therefore received a worst outcome scenario.

Good guys finish last...

Situation

XZ was a plastic surgeon who performed a breast enlargement on a middle aged lady. One year later he received papers notifying him that a suit was being brought against him for body disfigurement and emotional distress. The physician had a good service contract, so the case went to arbitration.

During arbitration the woman lost her temper, admitting that she was only responding to an attorney's ad stating that if you "felt" you had been wronged by a plastic surgeon then you could have a valid lawsuit. She stated that she wanted to be paid enough for her to get a liposuction and face lift.

Outcome

Papers were drawn up for a one dollar settlement, the physician signed them and breathed a sigh of relief.

Two years later a more aggressive attorney filed a suit for the same complaint and won. Statements made in arbitration are not admissible in a court of law, without both party's permission and she had not signed the original paperwork.

Discussion

- Always make sure that every legal agreement is signed, dated and witnessed.
- Just because you win a legal proceeding does not mean that is the end of it.
- If a patient accepts money for an issue they may still sue you again. Make sure that you get a "specific and general release agreement" and pay them some consideration for their undertaking never to pursue you again.

Resources:

- General release agreement
- Separation and release agreement
- www.PracticeWithoutFear.com

SAMPLE **Separation Agreement & General Release**

PERSONAL AND CONFIDENTIAL

Date:

To:

Re: Separation Agreement and General Release

Dear:

This letter proposes the following Separation Agreement and General Release (Agreement) between you and ______________________ (Company) regarding the terms of your separation from Company.

I. Background

A. You were employed by the Company as ____________________________. You and the Company have agreed to terminate your employment relationship on an amicable basis.

B. On the _____ day of ___________, 20__, your employment with the Company terminated.

II. Terms of Agreement

In order to effect the termination of your employment and to provide you with certain benefits that you would not otherwise be entitled to, you and the Company agree as follows:

A. This Agreement shall not be in any way construed as an admission by the Company that it has acted wrongfully with respect to you or any other person, or that you have any rights whatsoever against the Company.

B. Even if you do not sign this Agreement, the Company will pay you the compensation that you have earned through the date of your termination, any accrued vacation benefits, and [insert any appropriate profit sharing, etc. plan name here] in accordance with the terms and conditions of such plan. Similarly, even if you do not sign this Agreement, you will be offered benefits to which you are entitled under the Consolidated Omnibus Budget Reconciliation Act of 1985 ("COBRA"), and you retain all benefits under the Company's 401(k) Plan.

C. In exchange for the promises contained in this Agreement and release of claims as set forth below, and provided that you sign this agreement and return it to Company on or before the _____ day of ____________, 20__, and do not revoke this Agreement as set forth in Paragraph 15(d):

a. The Company will pay you a severance allowance in the amount of your current base monthly salary of _________ dollars ($) beginning on the _____ day of ____________, and ending on the _____ day of ____________ to be paid on a monthly basis and in accordance with the Company's normal payroll process.

b. The Company will pay for your medical coverage premiums (i.e., COBRA benefits) under the Company's Group Health Insurance Plan.

c. If you wish, the Company will pay for an outplacement service (to be selected by the Company) for services rendered in assisting you in locating another job, for a period of ____ months following the date of your termination or until you begin working for another employer, whichever occurs first. These payments are contingent upon your cooperation with the outplacement service and upon active efforts by you to locate another position.

D. In consideration of the promises contained in this Agreement, you agree:

a. On behalf of yourself and anyone claiming through you, irrevocably and unconditionally to release, acquit and forever discharge the Company and/or its parent corporation, subsidiaries, divisions, predecessors, successors and assigns, as well as their past and present officers, directors, employees, shareholders, trustees, joint venturers, partners, and anyone claiming through them (collectively referred to as Releasees), in their individual and/or corporate capacities, from any and all claims, liabilities, promises, actions, damages and the like, known or unknown, which you ever had against any of the Releasees arising out of or relating to your employment with the Company and/or the termination of your employment with the Company. Said claims include, but are not limited to: (1) employment discrimination (including claims of sex discrimination and/or sexual harassment) and retaliation under Title VII (42 U.S.C.A. 2000e etc.) and under 42 U.S.C.A. section 1981 and section 1983, age discrimination under the Age Discrimination in Employment Act (29 U.S.C.A. sections 621-634) as amended, and/or any other relevant state statutes or municipal ordinances; (2) disputed wages; (3) wrongful discharge and/or breach of any alleged employment contract; and (4) claims based on any tort, such as invasion of privacy, defamation, fraud and infliction of emotional distress.

b. That you shall not bring any legal action against any of the Releasees for any claim waived and released under this Agreement and that you represent and warrant that no such claim has been filed to date. You further agree that should you bring any type of administrative or legal action arising out of claims waived under this Agreement, you will bear all legal fees and costs, including those of the Releasees.

E. You agree to refer any and all reference checks to ______________________ and you know that any such references will be limited to confirmation of the dates of your employment and last position held. The obligation under this Paragraph is separable and any failure by the Company to perform the obligation in this Paragraph will only give rise to an action to enforce this Paragraph.

F. You agree that you will not, directly or indirectly, disclose the fact of and terms of this Agreement, including the severance benefits, to anyone other than your attorney, except to the extent such disclosure may be required for accounting or tax reporting purposes or as otherwise required by law.

G. This agreement shall be binding on the parties and upon their heirs, administrators, representatives, executors, successors and assigns and shall inure to their benefit and to that of their heirs, administrators, representatives, executors, successors and assigns.

H. On or before the _____ day of ____________, 20__, you will return to Company all of the Company's property in your possession including, but not limited to, customer lists, mailing lists, account information, samples, prototypes, price lists and pricing information, phone cards, cellular phone, automobile and all of the tangible and intangible property belonging to the Company and relating to your employment with the Company. You further represent and warrant that you have not retained any copies, electronic or otherwise, of such property.

I. You will cooperate fully with the Company in its defense of or other participation in any administrative, judicial or other proceeding arising from any charge, complaint or other action that has been or may be filed.

J. You will continue to comply with the terms of the Proprietary and Confidentiality Agreement between you and the Company, executed on the _____ day of ____________, 20__, and know and understand that the obligations contained in that agreement survive execution of this Agreement and your termination of employment. In particular, you shall not disclose any confidential or proprietary information (specifically including pricing, margins, key customer contacts and their profiles not generally known to the public) which you acquired as an employee of the Company to any other person or entity, or use such information in any manner that is detrimental to the interest of the Company. A copy of your Confidentiality Agreement is attached as Exhibit 1.

K. You agree that you will not make any comments relating to the Company or its employees which are critical, derogatory or which may tend to injure the business of the Company.

L. In the event that you breach any of your obligations under Paragraphs H through K, any outstanding obligations of the Company hereunder shall immediately terminate, and any payments previously made to you pursuant to Paragraph C shall be returned to the Company.

M. You also acknowledge that you have been informed pursuant to the federal Older Workers Benefit Protection Act of 1990 that:

a. You have the right to consult with an attorney before signing this Agreement;

b. You do not waive rights or claims under the federal Age Discrimination in Employment Act that may arise after the date this waiver is executed.

c. You have twenty-one (21) days from the date of this letter to consider this Agreement;

d. You have seven (7) days after signing this Agreement to revoke the Agreement, and the Agreement will not be effective until that revocation period has expired.

N. The provisions of this Agreement are severable. If any provision is held to be invalid or unenforceable, it shall not affect the validity or enforceability of any other provision.

O. This Agreement sets forth the entire agreement between you and the Company and supersedes any and all prior oral or written agreements or understandings between you and the Company concerning the subject matter of this Agreement. This Agreement may not be altered, amended or modified, except by a further written document signed by you and the Company.

P. You represent that you fully understand your right to review all aspects of this Agreement with an attorney of your choice, that you have had the opportunity to consult with an attorney of your choice, that you have carefully read and fully understand all the provisions of this Agreement and that you are freely, knowingly and voluntarily entering into this Separation Agreement and General Release. If you are willing to enter into this Agreement, please signify your acceptance in the space indicated below, and return to Company by the _____ day of ____________, 20__. As I noted earlier, this Agreement will not become effective, and none of the severance benefits in Paragraph 3 will be paid, until seven (7) days after the date you sign this Agreement.

PLEASE READ CAREFULLY. YOU ARE GIVING UP ANY LEGAL CLAIMS THAT YOU HAVE AGAINST THE COMPANY BY SIGNING THIS AGREEMENT.

Sincerely,

____

Signature and Title

Accepted and agreed to on this the _____ day of ____________, 20__.

_____________________________________ __________________

Signature of Employee Date

COMING SOON

Practice Without Fear - Case Studies

We need your help

Please send us in your stories of asset protection, liability reduction, malpractice nightmares, etc. Tell us what you did wrong, what you did right, what you should have done and what you learned. Please do not use your real name, unless you wish to. If we feature your story we will send you a copy of the book.

Contact: TobyUnwin@PracticeWithoutFear.com

Practice Without Fear 201

Practice Without Fear is an entry level book to teach any physician about asset protection and how to protect themselves. We'll be coming out with a more advanced version soon. It will be a 1,000 page book and written in conjunction with some of the best experts in law and finance.

Seminars

We will be holding seminars across the country. If you're interested in finding out more on how to reduce your liability and protect your assets then you need to attend.

- Learn more about Physician Liability reduction and Asset Protection
- Network with your peers
- Ask experts the questions that specifically pertain to you and your situation

Visit www.PracticeWithoutFear.com for more details

About the authors

Roger Murray M.D.

Roger Y. Murray, M.D. graduated from the Medical University of South Carolina in 1977, after which he did an internship in Internal Medicine and residency in Family Practice.

He became Board Certified in 1980, and recertified in 1987. From 1980-1981 he was the Emergency Room Physician at Florida Hospital in Altamonte, Florida. He has been in private practice in Altamonte Springs since 1981.

His interest in Phlebology started in 1987. Having been a speaker for Hoechst-Roussel on Peripheral Vascular Disease, (which deals with arterial disease of the legs) for five years, Dr. Murray wanted to know more about venous diseases of the legs. What started out as just attending a conference to expand his horizons, has developed into the passion of his professional life.

He studied extensively both at home and abroad for three years before actually beginning to practice Phlebology. He is now a member of The North American Society of Phlebology and Canadian Society of Phlebology and continues to lecture on both arterial and venous leg.

Roger has personal experience of losing assets after he went through a four year legal battle in a routine divorce case, the attorney's fees exceed $0.5 Million. His wife was awarded 80% of his assets. He wishes he knew then what he knows now.

He has practiced for over 25 years in the State of Florida.

He has never had a single malpractice case or complaint.

Toby Unwin M.B.A

Toby founded and sold one the few profitable Internet businesses in Europe, NetSearch™ Limited which provided Internet based headhunting services to recruitment firms and end users with a database of over 120M people. He retired aged 26.

Amongst other honorary positions he is also an Internet Strategy Consultant to United Nations affiliate organizations.

He is an acknowledged expert on asset protection and International business. He is often consulted by multi national corporations, high net worth individuals and performs consultancy work for extra national organizations.

Whilst he dislikes legal action he is extremely well prepared for the type of threats that unfortunately plague our society.

He has never lost a lawsuit anywhere in the World.

Consultancy

You can contact the authors at:
Dr.Murray@PracticeWithoutFear.com
TobyUnwin@PracticeWithoutFear.com or visit
www.PracticeWithoutFear.com

How to order more copies

www.PracticeWithoutFear.com
Volume discounts and books with your corporate branding are available.

Moving Forward

We hope that you have enjoyed this book and learned from it. It is a shame that the attitudes of a few unscrupulous attorneys and a very few patients have infected the public consciousness. People must start to take responsibility for their own actions and not look to others, or the state, to insulate them from their own responsibility.

Too often our legal system focuses on the medical outcome rather than any medical malpractice. The two should not be interchangeable. We urge you, any your patients to write to your political representatives(as physicians you should give them the actual names, email addresses, form letters and stamped, addressed envelopes), to pass the following reforms:

- Pass meaningful tort reform.
- Cap non-economic damages at $250,000 in lawsuits.
- Eliminate the joint and several liability provisions
- Modify the contingency fee system that allows attorneys to keep up to 40% of the monies awarded in lawsuits, plus all expenses. We believe the French standard of a 7% cap should be adopted.
- Have an independent arbitrator panel, of an equal amount of attorneys, physicians and the lay public, set legal damage awards.
- Allow for periodic payments of damages, rather than a lump sum.

Bibliography

Hide your assets and disappear – Edmund J. Pankau
Fugitive – Ken Abaygo
The tax haven report – Adam Starchild
Banking in silence – W.G. Hill
Advanced Fugitive – Ken Abaygo
International Fugitive – Ken Abaygo
The Paper Trip I – Eden Press
The Paper Trip II – Eden Press
The Paper Trip III – Eden Press
Bullet Proof Asset Protection – William S. Reed J.D.
International identity change – Newborn
Who are you – Scott French
The bumper book of bank applications – Patrick Torrent
Privacy and how to get it – Eden Press
How to Disappear in America – Eden Press
How to disappear completely and never be found – Doug Richmond
Part time diplomacy – James Basil-Hart
Above the law – Ambassador X
Everything about diplomatic passports, diplomatic status, honorary consulates and related matters – Global money consultants
Asset protection secrets – Arnold Goldstein
The Sovereign Individual – Lord Rees Mogg

Appendix

State Licensing Boards

Alabama State Board of Medical Examiners
Larry D. Dixon, Executive Administrator
P.O. Box 946
Montgomery, AL 36101-0946
(street address: 848 Washington Ave.)
(334) 242-4116 / Fax:(334) 242-4155
(800) 227-2606
www.albme.org

Alaska State Medical Board
Leslie A. Gallant, Executive Administrator
550 West Seventh Ave., Suite 1500
Anchorage, AK 99501
(907) 269-8163 / Fax:(907) 269-8196
http://www.dced.state.ak.us/occ/pmed.htm

Arizona Medical Board
Barry A. Cassidy, PhD, PA-C, Executive Director
9545 East Doubletree Ranch Road
Scottsdale, AZ 85258-5514
(480) 551-2700 / Fax: (480) 551-2704
www.bomex.org

Arizona Board of Osteopathic Examiners in Medicine and Surgery
Elaine LeTarte, Acting Executive Director
9535 East Doubletree Ranch Road
Scottsdale, AZ 85258-5539
(480) 657-7703 Fax (480) 657-7715
www.azosteoboard.org

Arkansas State Medical Board
Peggy P. Cryer, Executive Secretary
2100 Riverfront Dr.
Little Rock, AR 72202-1793
(501) 296-1802 / Fax:(501) 296-1805
www.armedicalboard.org

Medical Board of California
Ronald Joseph, Executive Director
1426 Howe Ave., Suite 54
Sacramento, CA 95825-3236
(916) 263-2389 / Fax:(916) 263-2387
(800) 633-2322
www.medbd.ca.gov

Osteopathic Medical Board of California
Linda J. Bergmann, Executive Director
2720 Gateway Oaks Dr., Suite 350
Sacramento, CA 95833-3500
(916) 263-3100 / Fax:(916) 263-3117
www.dca.ca.gov/osteopathic

Colorado Board of Medical Examiners
Susan Miller, Program Administrator
1560 Broadway, Suite 1300
Denver, CO 80202-5140
(303) 894-7690 / Fax:(303) 894-7692
www.dora.state.co.us/medical

Connecticut Medical Examining Board
Jeff Kardys, Board Liaison
P.O. Box 340308
Hartford, CT 06134-0308
(street address 410 Capitol Ave., MS13PHO)
(860) 509-7648 / Fax:(860) 509-7553
Licensing Information,(860) 509-7563
www.dph.state.ct.us

Delaware Board of Medical Practice
Gayle Franzolino, Interim Executive Director
P.O. Box 1401
Dover, DE 19903
(street address: 861 Silver Lake Blvd., Cannon Building, Suite 203, 19904)
(302) 739-4522 / Fax:(302) 739-2711
www.professionallicensing.state.de.us

District of Columbia Board of Medicine
James R. Granger, Jr., Executive Director
825 North Capital Street, NE, 2nd Floor
Washington, DC 20002
(202) 442-9200/ Fax: (202) 442-9431
dchealth.dc.gov

Florida Board of Medicine
Larry McPherson, Esq., Executive Director
Department of Health
4052 Bald Cypress Way, BIN #C03
Tallahassee, FL 32399-3253
(850) 245-4131/ Fax:(850) 488-9325
www.doh.state.fl.us

Florida Board of Osteopathic Medicine
Pamela King, Executive Director
4052 Bald Cypress Way, BIN C06
Tallahassee, FL 32399-1753
(850) 245-4161 / Fax:(850) 487-9874
www.doh.state.fl.us

Georgia Composite State Board of Medical Examiners
Karen Mason, Executive Director
2 Peachtree Street, NW, 36th Floor
Atlanta, GA 30303
(404) 656-3913 / Fax:(404) 656-9723
www.medicalboard.state.ga.us

Guam Board of Medical Examiners
Teresita L.G. Villagomez, Acting Administrator
Health Professionals Licensing
1304 East Sunset Blvd.
Hagatna, GU 96913
(011) 671-475-0251 / Fax:(011) 671-477-4733

Hawaii Board of Medical Examiners
Constance Cabral, Executive Officer
Dept. of Commerce & Consumer Affairs
P.O. Box 3469

Honolulu, HI 96813
(street address: 1010 Richards St., 96813)
(808) 586-3000 / Fax:(808) 586-2874
www.state.hi.us

Idaho State Board of Medicine
Nancy Kerr, Executive Director
1755 Westgate Drive, Suite 140,
Boise, ID 83704
(street address: 83704)
(208) 327-7000 / Fax:(208) 327-7005
www.bom.state.id.us

Illinois Department of Professional Regulation
Aurelia Pucinski, Director
(Discipline)
James R. Thompson Center
100 W. Randolph St., Suite 9-300
Chicago, IL 60601
(312) 814-4500 / Fax:(312) 814-1837
www.dpr.state.il.us

Alicia Purchase, Board Liaison
(Licensure)
320 W. Washington St., 3rd Floor
Springfield, IL 62786
(217) 785-0800 / Fax:(217) 524-2169
www.dpr.state.il.us

Indiana Health Professions Bureau
Lisa R. Hayes, J.D., Executive Director
402 W. Washington St., Room 041
Indianapolis, IN 46204
(317) 232-2960 / Fax:(317) 233-4236
www.ai.org/hpb

Iowa State Board of Medical Examiners
Ann Mowery, Ph.D., Executive Director
400 Southwest Eighth Street, Suite C
Des Moines, IA 50309-4686

(515) 281-5171 / Fax:(515) 242-5908
www.docboard.org/ia/ia_home.htm

Kansas Board of Healing Arts
Lawrence Buening Jr., J.D., Executive Director
235 South Topeka Blvd.
Topeka, KS 66603-3068
(785) 296-7413 / Fax:(785) 296-0852
www.ksbha.org

Kentucky Board of Medical Licensure
C. William Schmidt, Executive Director
Hurstbourne Office Park
310 Whittington Parkway, Suite 1B
Louisville, KY 40222-4916
(502) 429-8046 / Fax:(502) 429-9923
www.state.ky.us/agencies/kbml

Louisiana State Board of Medical Examiners
John B. Bobear M.D., Executive Director
P.O. Box 30250
New Orleans, LA 70190-0250
(street address: 630 Camp St., 70130)
(504) 568-6820 / Fax:(504) 568-8893
www.lsbme.org

Maine Board of Licensure in Medicine
Randal C. Manning, Executive Director
137 State House Station (U.S. mail)
2 Bangor Street, 2nd Floor (delivery service)
Augusta, ME 04333
(207) 287-3601 / Fax:(207) 287-6590
www.docboard.org/me/me_home.htm

Maine Board of Osteopathic Licensure
Susan E. Strout, Executive Secretary
142 State House Station
Augusta, ME 04333-0142
(207) 287-2480 (207) 287-3015
www.docboard.org/me-osteo

Maryland Board of Physician Quality Assurance
C. Irving Pinder, Executive Director
P.O. Box 2571
Baltimore, MD 21215-0095
(street address: 4201 Patterson Ave., third floor, 21215)
(410) 764-4777 / Fax:(410) 358-2252
(800) 492-6836
www.bpqa.state.md.us

Massachusetts Board of Registration in Medicine
Nancy Achin Sullivan, Executive Director
560 Harrison Ave. Suite G-4
Boston, MA 02118
(617) 654-9800 / Fax:(617) 451-9568
(800) 377-0550
www.massmedboard.org

Michigan Board of Medicine
Ann Marie Pischea, Licensing Director
P.O. Box 30670
Lansing, MI 48909-8170
(street address: 611 W. Ottawa St, 1st floor, 48933
(517) 373-6873 / Fax:(517) 373-2179
www.michigan.gov/cis

Michigan Board of Osteopathic Medicine and Surgery
Ann Marie Pischea, Licensing Director
P.O. Box 30670
Lansing, MI 48909-8170
(street address: 611 W. Ottawa St, 1st floor, 48933
(517) 373-6873 / Fax:(517) 373-2179
www.michigan.gov/cis

Minnesota Board of Medical Practice
Robert A. Leach, J.D., Executive Director
University Park Plaza
2829 University Ave. SE, Suite 400
Minneapolis, MN 55414-3246
(612) 617-2130 / Fax:(612) 617-2166

Hearing impaired 1-800-627-3529
www.bmp.state.mn.us

Mississippi State Board of Medical Licensure
W. Joseph Burnett, M.D., Director
1867 Crane Ridge Drive, Suite 200B
Jackson, MS 39216
(601) 987-3079 / Fax:(601) 987-4159
www.msbml.state.ms.us

Missouri State Board of Registration for the Healing Arts
Tina M. Steinman, Executive Director
3605 Missouri Blvd.
Jefferson City, MO 65109
(street address: 3605 Missouri Blvd., 65109)
(573) 751-0098 / Fax:(573) 751-3166
www.ecodev.state.mo.us/pr/healarts/

Montana Board of Medical Examiners
Jeannie Worsech, Executive Director
P.O. Box 200513
Helena, MT 59620-0513
(406) 841-2300 / Fax: (406) 841-2363
Discovering Montana

Nebraska Board of Medicine and Surgery
Health and Human Services
Regulation and Licensure Credentialing Division
Becky Wisell, Section Administrator
P.O. Box 94986
Lincoln, NE 68509-4986
(402) 471-2118 / Fax:(402) 471-3577
www.hhs.state.ne.us/

Nevada State Board of Medical Examiners
Larry D. Lessly, J.D., Executive Director
1105 terminal Way, Suite 301
Reno, NV 89502
(775) 688-2559 / Fax:(775) 688-2321
www.medboard.nv.gov

Nevada State Board of Osteopathic Medicine
Larry J. Tarno, D.O., Executive Director
2860 E. Flamingo Rd., Suite G
Las Vegas, NV 89121
(702) 732-2147 / Fax:(702) 732-2079
www.osteo.state.nv.us

New Hampshire Board of Medicine
Penny Taylor, Administrator
2 Industrial Park Drive, Suite 8
Concord, NH 03301-8520
(603) 271-1203 / Fax:(603) 271-6702
complaints (800) 780-4757
www.state.nh.us/medicine

New Jersey State Board of Medical Examiners
William V. Roeder, Executive Director
P.O. Box 183
Trenton, NJ 08625-0183
(609) 826-7100 / Fax:(609) 826-7117
www.state.nj.us/lps/ca/medical.htm#bme5

New Mexico State Board of Medical Examiners
Charlotte Kinney, Executive Director
491 Old Santa Fe Trail, Lamy Building, 2nd Floor
Santa Fe, NM 87501
(505) 827-5022 / Fax:(505) 827-7377
www.state.nm.us/nmbme

New Mexico Board of Osteopathic Medical Examiners
Liz Z. Montoya, Executive Director
2055 S. Pacheco, Suite 400
Santa Fe, NM 87504
(505) 476-7120 / Fax:(505) 476-7095
www.rld.state.nm.us

New York State Board for Medicine (Licensure)
Thomas J. Monahan, Executive Secretary
89 Washington Avenue, 2nd Floor, West Wing
Albany, NY 12234

(518) 474-3817 Ext. 560 / Fax:(518) 486-4846
www.op.nysed.gov

New York State Board for Professional Medical Conduct (Discipline)
Dennis J. Graziano, Executive Director
Department of Health
Office of Professional Medical Conduct
433 River St., Suite 303
Troy, NY 12180-2299
(518) 402-0855 / Fax:(518) 402-0866
www.health.state.ny.us/

North Carolina Medical Board
Andrew W. Watry, M.P.A., Executive Director
P.O. Box 20007
Raleigh, NC 27619
(919) 326-1100 / Fax:(919) 326-1130
www.ncmedboard.org

North Dakota State Board of Medical Examiners
Rolf P. Sletten, JD, Executive Secretary/Treasurer
City Center Plaza
418 E. Broadway, Suite 12
Bismarck, ND 58501
(701) 328-6500 / Fax:(701) 328-6505
www.ndbomex.com

Northern Mariana Islands
Medical Profession Licensing Board
Juanet S. Crisostomo, Office Manager
P.O. Box 501458, CK
Saipan, MP 96950
(670) 664-4811 / Fax:(670) 664-4813
www.saipan.com/gov

Back to Top

State Medical Board of Ohio
Thomas A. Dilling, J.D., Executive Director
77 S. High St., 17th Floor
Columbus, OH 43215-6127

(614) 466-3934 / Fax:(614) 728-5946
(800) 554-7717
www.state.oh.us/med/

Oklahoma State Board of Medical Licensure and Supervision
Lyle Kelsey, C.A.E., Executive Director
P.O. Box 18256
Oklahoma City, OK 73118
(405) 848-6841 / Fax:(405) 848-8240
(800) 381-4519
www.osbmls.state.ok.us

Oklahoma State Board of Osteopathic Examiners
Gary R. Clark, Executive Director
4848 N. Lincoln Blvd, Suite 100
Oklahoma City, OK 73105-3321
(405) 528-8625 / Fax:(405) 557-0653
www.docboard.org

Oregon Board of Medical Examiners
Kathleen Haley, J.D., Executive Director
1500 SW First Avenue, 620 Crown Plaza
Portland, OR 97201-5826
(503) 229-5770 / Fax:(503) 229-6543
www.bme.state.or.us

Pennsylvania State Board of Medicine
Joanne Troutman, Administrator
P.O. Box 2649
Harrisburg, PA 17105-7769
(717) 787-2381 / Fax:(717) 787-7769
www.dos.state.pa.us

Pennsylvania State Board of Osteopathic Medicine
Gina K. Bittner, Administrator
P.O. Box 2649
Harrisburg, PA 17105-2649
(street address: 124 Pine St., 17101)
(717) 783-4858 / Fax:(717) 787-7769
www.dos.state.pa.us

Board of Medical Examiners of Puerto Rico
Pablo Valentin-Torres, Esq, Executive Director
P.O. Box 13969
San Juan, PR 00908
(787) 782-8949 / Fax:(787) 792-4436

Rhode Island Board of Medical Licensure and Discipline
Bruce W. McIntyre, J.D., Interim Chief Administrator
Department of Health
Cannon Building, Room 205
Three Capitol Hill
Providence, RI 02908-5097
(401) 222-3855 / Fax:(401) 222-2158
www.docboard.org/ri/main.htm

South Carolina Board of Medical Examiners
Department of Labor, Licensing and Regulation
John D. Volmer, Board Administrator
110 Centerview Drive, Suite 202
Columbia, SC 29210-1289
(803) 896-4500 / Fax:(803) 896-4515
www.llr.state.sc.us/pol/medical

South Dakota State Board of Medical and Osteopathic Examiners
L. Paul Jensen, Executive Secretary
1323 S. Minnesota Ave.
Sioux Falls, SD 57105
(605) 334-8343 / Fax:(605) 336-0270
www.state.sd.us/dcr/medical

Tennessee Board of Medical Examiners
Rosemarie Otto, Executive Director
425 5th Ave. North, 1st Floor, Cordell Hull Building
Nashville, TN 37247-1010
(615) 532-3202 / Fax:(615) 253-4484
www.state.tn.us/health

Tennessee Board of Osteopathic Examiners
Rosemarie Otto, Executive Director
425 5th Ave. North, 1st Floor, Cordell Hull Building

Nashville, TN 37247-1010
(615) 532-3202/ Fax:(615) 253-4484
(888) 310-4650
www.state.tn.us/health

Texas State Board of Medical Examiners
Donald W. Patrick, M.D., J.D., Executive Director
P.O. Box 2018
Austin, TX 78768-2018
(512) 305-7010/Fax: (512) 305-7008
Disciplinary Hotline (800) 248-4062
Consumer Complaint Hotline (800) 201-9353
www.tsbme.state.tx.us

Utah Department of Commerce
Div. of Occupational & Professional Licensure
Physicians Licensing Board
Craig J. Jackson, R.Ph.
160 E 300 South, 84102, Heber M. Wells Building, 4th Floor
Salt Lake City, UT 84114
(801) 530-6628 / Fax:(801) 530-6511
www.dopl.utah.gov

Utah Department of Commerce
Div. of Occupational & Professional Licensure
Board of Osteopathic Medicine
Diana T. Baker, Bureau Manager
160 E 300 South, 84102, Heber M. Wells Building, 4th Floor
Salt Lake City, UT 84114
(801) 530-6628 / Fax:(801) 530-6511
www.dopl.utah.gov

Vermont Board of Medical Practice
John Howland, Interim Executive Director
108 Cherry Street
Burlington, VT 05402-0070
(802) 657-4220 / Fax:(802) 657-4227
www.healthyvermonters.info

Vermont Board of Osteopathic Physicians and Surgeons
Jessica Porter, Director, Office of Professional Regulation
26 Terrace Street, Drawer 09
Montpelier, VT 05609-1106
(802) 828-2373 / Fax:(802) 828-2465
www.sec.state.vt.us

Virgin Islands Board of Medical Examiners
Lydia Scott, Executive Assistant
Department of Health
48 Sugar Estate
St. Thomas, VI 00802
(340) 774-0117/ Fax:(340) 777-4001

Virginia Board of Medicine
William L. Harp, M.D., Executive Director
6603 W. Broad St., 5th Floor
Richmond, VA 23230-1717
(804) 662-9908 / Fax:(804) 662-9517
www.dhp.state.va.us/

Washington Medical Quality Assurance Commission
Doron N. Maniece, Executive Director
Department of Health
P.O. Box 47866
Olympia, WA 98504-7866
(360) 236-4788 / Fax:(360) 586-4573
www.doh.wa.gov

Washington State Board of Osteopathic Medicine and Surgery
Robert Nicoloff, Executive Director
Department of Health
P.O Box 47870
Olympia, WA 98504-7870
(360) 236-4943 / Fax:(360) 236-2406
www.doh.wa.gov

West Virginia Board of Medicine
Ronald D. Walton, Executive Director
101 Dee Drive

Charleston, WV 25311
(304) 558-2921 / Fax:(304) 558-2084
www.wvdhhr.org/wvbom

West Virginia Board of Osteopathy
Cheryl Schreiber, Executive Secretary
334 Penco Rd.
Weirton, WV 26062
(304) 723-4638 / Fax:(304) 723-2877
www.state.wv.us/bdosteo

Wisconsin Medical Examining Board
Department of Regulation and Licensing
Deanna Zychomski, Bureau Director
1400 E. Washington Ave.
Madison, WI 53703
(608) 266-2112 / Fax:(608) 261-7083
www.drl.state.wi.us

Wyoming Board of Medicine
Carole Shotwell, J.D., Executive Secretary
211 W. 19th St., Colony Bldg., 2nd floor
Cheyenne, WY 82002
(307) 778-7053 / Fax:(307) 778-2069
wyomedboard.state.wy.us

NOTES

NOTES

Printed in the United States
20992LVS00001B/31-80

9 780972 981408